The Power of Thetis

Laura M. Slatkin

The Power of Thetis

Allusion and Interpretation in the *Iliad*

University of California Press

Berkeley   Los Angeles   Oxford

University of California Press
Berkeley and Los Angeles, California

University of California Press, Ltd.
Oxford, England

Library of Congress Cataloging-in-Publication
Data

Slatkin, Laura M.
    The power of Thetis : allusion and inter-
pretation in the Iliad / Laura M. Slatkin.
      p. cm.
    Includes bibliographical references and index.
    ISBN 0-520-07251-0
    1. Homer. Iliad. 2. Thetis (Greek mythol-
ogy) in literature. 3. Achilles (Greek mythology)
in literature. 4. Trojan War in literature.
I. Title.
PA4037.S49   1991   91-6712
883'.01——dc20   CIP

Printed in the United States of America
9 8 7 6 5 4 3 2 1

TO C.A.S. AND R.L.S.

AND

TO THE MEMORY OF C.E.S.

Contents

Acknowledgments

Acknowledgments are the ultimate form of allusion. To record my gratitude to the individuals named here is to evoke with renewed pleasure the conversations from which I learned so much and the friendships out of which they arose. For a short book, then, this one boasts, happily, a long list of debts.

Like its subject Thetis, this book arrived at its present form after several stages of metamorphosis. Throughout all of them, Sara Bershtel, Margaret Carroll, and Amy Johnson, together with Pat Easterling, John H. Finley Jr., Gregory Nagy, and Richard Sacks have been heroic in their efforts to clarify my thinking about the *Iliad* and more. Suffice it to say allusively here that their wisdom and their fortifying affection have profoundly sustained and rewarded my work; in a real sense, they have been my collaborators.

The study began to take shape in 1976 while I was teaching at the University of California at Santa Cruz and owes much to the sympathetic interest of my colleagues and students from those incomparably stimulating days, most especially to the indispensable, bracing, and illuminating criticisms of Norman O. Brown. Over recent years, Nicole Loraux has been an unfailingly responsive interlocutor, for whose commitment to this study I am deeply grateful; her challenging insight into the issues addressed here and the breadth of her perspective on them have enriched my understanding of the material and guided me to see a larger context for its meaning. With characteristic generosity and care, Richard Janko read the manuscript in all its versions and has contributed countless valuable suggestions; without his warm support and kindly prodding, this book would not exist. Helen Bacon, Andrée Hayum, Seth Schein, and Froma Zeitlin have been, as always, forthright, astute, and patient critics, as have Dale Sinos, Robert Tannenbaum, and James Zetzel; I have benefitted from their compelling questions and judicious advice. For their welcome encouragement and perceptive comments, I think gratefully of the late Steele Commager, and of Harry Berger, Jr., Ann Bergren, Lillian Doherty, Helene Foley, Kathy Eden, Nancy Felson-Rubin, Douglas Frame, Michele Hannoosh, Jinyo Kim, Katherine King, Gary Miles, Michael Nagler, Holly Nagy, Joseph Russo, Rose Slatkin, and Kate Toll.

Most recently, the University of California Press has provided a return to the hospitable West Coast spirit of collective endeavor. For this I thank Richard Holway, whose knowledge of archaic Greek poetry and early enthusiasm for this study helped to get the project under way, and particularly Doris Kretschmer, who, with extraordinary editorial acumen, grace, and efficiency, made the rest of the way seem effortless. The Hesiodic genealogy was right: Doris did bring forth Thetis! I am greatly indebted to Mary Lamprech for expertly and scrupulously seeing the whole project through to completion, with her distinctive combination of rigor and reassurance, and to Marian Shotwell, whose thoughtful copyediting improved the manuscript. I am indebted as well to The American Council of Learned Societies for a fellowship, and to the Society of Fellows in the Humanities at Columbia University for a Mellon fellowship, both of which advanced the evolution of this book.

Above all, I wish to express my appreciation to Carole Slatkin for her invaluable solidarity on all fronts, and to Regina Slatkin for her heartening, optimistic counsel and her unstinting assistance on every aspect of this study from its inception, and for her erudite and invigorating curiosity about all matters Homeric. Whatever is worthwhile in the following pages is intended as a devoted tribute to them, and to the memory of my father.

Preface

As every era finds its own reasons for reading the *Iliad* and the *Odyssey* and discovers its own meaning in them, so it must participate in the ongoing process of discriminating Homeric thought—attitudes, values, ideology—from its own, rather than assimilating Homer to itself. The attempt to establish a context within which to read Homeric poetry must naturally draw on the indispensable efforts of archaeologists, historians, anthropologists, linguists, and specialists in ancient religion in order to provide appropriate bearings for analysis. This is obvious enough when we consider social and political institutions, economic configurations, or technology, areas in which the differences between our world and that of early Greece are apparent. Modes of perception and cognition, as reflected in literature, are more difficult to distinguish and identify.

The challenge to define as fully as possible the cultural environment in which a work of literature was produced presents itself with every examination of an ancient text. In the case of the extraordinarily complex phenomenon of Attic drama the task is perhaps facilitated by the survival of more complete documentation about the conditions, if not of its genesis, at least of its evolution and reception during the fifth century, as well as by contemporary commentary on it, as in the plays of Aristophanes. Drama, moreover, has continued to flourish as an art form with many of its conventions intact, and through our own experience of it in practice we appreciate much about how it realizes its aesthetic effects and meaning. Still, modern understanding of ancient drama is handicapped by ignorance of many of its integral features, such as music and dance. It is true nonetheless that readers of these works offer powerful and stimulating analyses of them; and it is by no means certain that if we were suddenly to find ourselves enlightened about ancient music and choreography we would need to alter our readings of the plays in a radical way. But a new awareness of these dimensions would entitle us to reconsider the plays interpretively, because it would mean that we would be able to hear and see them as their audiences did, to gauge more responsively the scope and complexity of their achievement.

Is there anything comparable that, as readers of Homer, we do not "hear" and "see"? The researches of Milman Parry and Albert Lord and others who have studied the mechanics and artistry of Homeric verse making have pioneered an awareness of its essential oral characteristics and altered our perception of the bases of its formal structure. Formulas, type-scenes, repeated episodes, have been fruitfully mapped; but the oral, traditional poet depends as well on other compositional techniques and resources alien to a literate culture, which are crucial to an understanding of the meaning of his poem.

Direct attention needs to be paid to the oral poet's orchestration of the mythology out of which his narrative is composed. The poet, it appears, constructs his narrative using myths that are not related in full, but only in part. Why should this be so? Is he inventing, but abridging, limiting the compass of his inventions? Is he attempting novelties and abandoning them unelaborated? Are these preparatory sketches awaiting further development? How are we to understand the poet's use of those fragments within the larger story?

The mythological corpus on which the poet draws, taken together, constitutes an internally logical and coherent system, accessible as such to the audience. The poet inherits as his repertory a system, extensive and flexible, whose components are familiar, in their manifold variant forms, to his listeners. For an audience that knows the mythological range of each character, divine or human—not only through this epic song but through other songs, epic and nonepic—the poet does not spell out the myth in its entirety but locates a character within it through allusion or oblique reference.

He thereby incorporates into his narrative another discourse, one that makes its appearance on the surface of the poem through oblique references, ellipses, or digressions, evoking for his audience themes that orient or supplement the events of the poem in particular ways. What becomes instrumental in this mode of composi-

tion is not only what the poet articulates by way of bringing a given myth (with its associated themes) into play,
in relation to his narrative, but also what is left unsaid;
for his audience would hear this as well.

In the continuously reversible shift of emphasis from
explicit to implicit meaning, how does the poet activate
the implicit? For an audience to whom this fundamental
compositional resource is foreign or to whom the myths
in their essential multivalence, flexibility, and systema-
ticity are unfamiliar, the task of hearing as Homer's audience did requires the apparently paradoxical task of
listening for what is unspoken.

Abbreviations

AuA	*Antike und Abendland*
AJP	*American Journal of Philology*
BICS	*Bulletin of the Institute of Classical Studies of the University of London*
BSL	*Bulletin de la Société de Linguistique de Paris*
CQ	*Classical Quarterly*
CW	*The Classical World*
GRBS	*Greek, Roman, and Byzantine Studies*
HSCP	*Harvard Studies in Classical Philology*
JHS	*Journal of Hellenic Studies*
MH	*Museum Helveticum*
POxy.	*Oxyrhynchus Papyri*
RE	*Paulys Real-Encyclopädie der classischen Altertumswissenschaft*
RhM	*Rheinisches Museum*
RHR	*Revue de l'Histoire des Religions*
TAPA	*Transactions and Proceedings of the American Philological Association*
YCS	*Yale Classical Studies*
ZPE	*Zeitschrift für Papyrologie und Epigraphik*

Introduction

The Homeric poems, as I hope to show, constitute acts of interpretation as well as acts of creation. The elucidation of their oral nature has taught us to look at Homeric composition not as a matter of rigidly prescribed transmission of inviolate requirements, but as a choice among alternative arrangements of fundamental compositional elements—formulas, diction, "themes," type-scenes—that allow for modification within established contours.[1] The process of participating in a poetic

---

1. Milman Parry's pioneering studies of the oral nature of the poems are reprinted and translated in Adam Parry's edition of his father's collected papers, published as *The Making of Homeric Verse* (Oxford, 1971); the fullest exposition of M. Parry and Albert Lord's seminal discoveries based on their fieldwork in Yugoslavia on living oral epic is in Lord's *The Singer of Tales* (Cambridge, Mass., 1960; reprint, New York, 1965). On "theme," the term by which Lord, following Parry, designated "the groups of ideas regularly used in telling a tale," see Lord's "Composition by Theme in Homer and Southslavic Epos," *TAPA* 82 (1951): 71–80, and his *Singer of Tales,* 68–98. On the dynamics of the oral poet's choice, Lord's writings are fundamental; see *Singer of Tales,* 13–29, esp. 98–123. Significant contributions to an understanding of particular aspects of the process have been numerous. Among

tradition, far from being a simple matter of inflexible dependence on antecedents, has emerged, on the contrary, as a process of selection at every stage.

On another level, but analogously, I propose, the *Iliad* and the *Odyssey* interpret the mythological material they inherit. As we shall see, they select not only from among different myths—combining those chosen into a

---

them one might cite, as a sample, the studies of A. Hoekstra, *Homeric Modifications of Formulaic Prototypes: Studies in the Development of Greek Epic Diction* (Amsterdam, 1964); J. Russo, "The Structural Formula in Homeric Verse," *YCS* 20 (1966): 217–40; J. B. Hainsworth, *The Flexibility of the Homeric Formula* (Oxford, 1968); M. Nagler, *Spontaneity and Tradition: A Study in the Oral Art of Homer* (Berkeley, 1974); M. Edwards, "Some Stylistic Notes on *Iliad* XVIII," *AJP* 89 (1968): 257–83; N. Postlethwaite, "Formula and Formulaic: Some Evidence from the Homeric Hymns," *Phoenix* 33 (1979): 1–18; R. Janko, *Homer, Hesiod and the Hymns: Diachronic Development in Epic Diction* (Cambridge, 1982); and M. Cantilena, *Ricerche sulla dizione epica* (Rome, 1982). R. Sacks, *The Traditional Phrase in Homer: Two Studies in Form, Meaning, and Interpretation* (Leiden, 1987), contributes an important discussion of the significance of context as a factor in the adaptability of traditional phraseology. On the modification of structural elements beyond the epithet system—motifs, "themes," or type-scenes (first examined in detail by W. Arend, *Die typischen Szenen bei Homer* [Berlin, 1933])—instructive works are many, including (in addition to those of Lord) B. Fenik, *Typical Battle Scenes in the* Iliad: *Studies in the Narrative Technique of Homeric Battle Description,* Hermes Einzelschriften 21 (Wiesbaden, 1968); D. Lohmann, *Die Komposition der Reden in der* Ilias (Berlin, 1970); T. Krischer, *Formale Konventionen der homerischen Epik* (Munich, 1971); C. P. Segal, *The Theme of the Mutilation of the Corpse in the* Iliad (Leiden, 1971); M. Edwards, "Type-scenes and Homeric Hospitality," *TAPA* 105 (1975): 51–72; as well as Nagler, *Spontaneity and Tradition.*

narrative within which certain central concerns illustrated by the myths are allowed full development—but
also from among different variants and aspects of a
single myth. As with rearrangements of formulas or
themes, alternative combinations of the features of a
myth are possible and equally legitimate, the choices
serving to reveal the framework imposed on its subject
matter by traditional genre requirements of heroic epic.[2]

But just as an individual formula implies a system of
formulaic usage—in each instance expresses not only its
individual "essential idea" but a principle of "formular-
ity"[3]—and just as any type-scene involves a recognized

2. Homeric epic, in its pan-Hellenic ambition, tends, for example, to exclude overt reference to distinctly local religious phenomena. As G. Nagy has shown in *The Best of the Achaeans* (Baltimore, 1979), elements in myth that refer to hero-cult are abridged
or suppressed in the epic narrative. See D. Sinos, *Achilles, Patroklos, and the Meaning of* Philos (Innsbruck, 1980), esp. 13–36,
47–52, for further elucidation of the consequences of this restric-
tion in the *Iliad* and for the manner in which Homeric poetry
"offers us clear proof by way of dictional analysis that its epic tradition does indeed contain elemental vestiges of cult and references to the heroes of cult in a manner necessarily modified to fit
the strict generic ordering of the language of epic" (15).

3. M. Parry's definition of the formula, given first in *L'épithète
traditionelle dans Homère* (Paris, 1928), was restated in "Studies in
the Epic Technique of Oral Versemaking," *HSCP* 41 (1930) as "a
group of words which is regularly employed under the same metri-
cal conditions, to express a given essential idea" (80). See Cantilena, *Dizione epica,* 36–73, for a balanced recent appraisal of the
major contributions to the debate about the nature of the formula.
For evaluations of the limitations of Parry's definition, with discussion of the general problem of definition and terminology, see
the papers in B. Stolz and R. Shannon, eds., *Oral Theory and the*

pattern, so, I will argue, a particular version of a myth is part of a larger whole that invites shaping, focusing, and integrating within a narrative structure, but that, however partially represented, can be invoked in all its dimensions. The epic audience's knowledge of the alternative possibilities allows the poet to build his narrative by deriving meaning not only from what the poem includes but from what it conspicuously excludes. A telling instance of this is the *Iliad*'s treatment of the Judgment of Paris. Presupposed by the poem and implicit in its plot, where it underlies divine as well as human alignments,[4] the Judgment of Paris would, however, remain an obscure reference, occurring as it does in a single allusion at the end of the poem (24.25–30)—if we were not able to look to sources outside Homer to recover the content of the myth and thus to appreciate the *Iliad*'s

---

Formula (Ann Arbor, Mich., 1976) by P. Kiparsky (pp. 73–104), J. Russo (pp. 31–54), and G. Nagy (pp. 239–257, now rewritten in id., *Greek Mythology and Poetics* [Ithaca, N.Y., 1990], 18–35); also A. Parry's introduction to *The Making of Homeric Verse,* esp. xxii–lxii. M. Edwards, "Homer and the Oral Tradition: The Formula, Part I," *Oral Tradition* 1/2 (1986): 171–230, and "Part II," *Oral Tradition* 3/1–2 (1988): 11–60, provide a judicious survey of the vast bibliography on the formula. For fundamental considerations of the relationship of a given formula to the larger compositional system, see Lord, *Singer of Tales,* 30–67, esp. 36–45 and 65–66; and the far-reaching generative approach of M. Nagler, "Towards a Generative View of the Oral Formula," *TAPA* 98 (1967): 269–311; as well as id., *Spontaneity and Tradition,* esp. chaps. 1 and 2.

4. See M. Davies, "The Judgement of Paris and *Iliad* XXIV," *JHS* 101 (1981): 56–62.

particular use and placement of it.[5] The epic can high-light or suppress attributes associated with a particular character, allowing their meaning to be colored by the specific narrative context, thus revising or manipulating its audience's expectations. And, in a complementary movement, it can appropriate the resonance of mytho-logical variants that the narrative context may not ex-plicitly accommodate. In adapting specific features in this way, the poem acts traditionally; it does not violate *tradition* (although it may be violating one particular tra-dition) but remains within it, exploiting its possibilities and using *traditionality* as an instrument of meaning.[6]

The discovery that the dynamics of selection and combination, modification and revision, are intrinsic to participation in an oral poetic tradition—that is, are tra-ditional operations themselves—applies, as I will argue in the present study, to the relationship the epic has with the mythology that is its medium, from which it derives both its identity as part of a system and its distinctive individuality. But if one suggests that modifications of formula, phrase, or type-scene find an analogy in the

5. See K. Reinhardt's important "Das Parisurteil," in *Tradition und Geist* (Göttingen, 1960), 16–36, first published as vol. 11 of *Wissenschaft und Gegenwart* (Frankfurt, 1938).

6. How enlightening an awareness of this process can be is powerfully demonstrated by the work of J. Th. Kakridis, *Homeric Researches* (Lund, 1949), whose analyses of the adaptation of motifs are informed by close familiarity with modern Greek folktale and song-making traditions; see in particular pp. 1–42, 106–48.

poem's handling of mythological variants, it is important to stress that no aboriginal prototype of a myth exists that can claim priority over other versions.[7]

This study will examine the processes by which Homeric epic draws on the full mythological range of each character in the development of that character's role and its relation to the poem's central ideas. An especially revealing example is the figure of Thetis. Her role in the *Iliad* (which has not previously been the subject of any special critical scrutiny) presents a number of enduringly enigmatic and apparently contradictory features that need to be considered in any interpretive approach to the poem, especially because the poem's use of her has important implications for its view of its principal character, Achilles, and hence of its dominant themes. The *Iliad*'s treatment of Thetis offers a crucial instance of the way in which its narrative incorporates traditional material from mythology that does not overtly reflect the subject matter of heroic poetry. To what end does it do so? How does the resonance of this material contribute a wider context and meaning to the *Iliad*'s central themes? Such a study thus aims to make a contribution to Homeric poetics, in that unraveling the functional identity of a figure like Thetis leads necessarily to the larger enterprise of determining what is and is not com-

7. As has been most effectively illustrated by Claude Lévi-Strauss's meticulous analyses; in *The Raw and the Cooked* (New York, 1969; reprint, 1975), see especially his discussion of the essential "multiplicity" of myths at pp. 12ff., 199ff., 332ff. See as well M. Detienne, *Dionysus mis à mort* (Paris, 1977), 23ff.

patible with Homeric epic's definition of its subject matter and realm of function—its boundaries as a genre. In
pursuing this inquiry, it will be useful to compare how
features of Thetis's mythology are exploited by independently inherited poetic traditions, such as those of
lyric poetry and the Epic Cycle.

In defining Thetis through a selective presentation of
her mythology, the *Iliad* makes explicit, emphatic use of
her attributes as a nurturing mother—a *kourotrophos*—
and protector. To put it another way, this aspect of
Thetis's mythology—her maternal, protective power—
which is adapted by the *Iliad,* makes possible one of the
poem's central ideas: the vulnerability of even the greatest of the heroes. Semidivine as Achilles is, death is inevitable even for him. At the same time, as we shall see,
the *Iliad* returns us to Thetis's role in the theogonic
myth of succession. In its superbly overdetermined econ-
omy, the *Iliad* shapes Thetis as thoroughly from the perspective of its hero's response and ultimate mortal concerns as it delineates his human dilemma against the
dimension of a particular divine genealogy. The formal
accommodation of Thetis's mythology within epic is recapitulated in the shape of the Homeric *Iliad.* In defining
Thetis, therefore, the poem defines itself.

The discovery of the oral and traditional nature of the
Homeric poems, and our increased grasp of the extraordinary complexity and refinement of their oral evolution, has prompted the suggestion that we need a new
poetics in order to read them. J. A. Notopoulos, for example, whose work represented an important contribu-

tion to the early discussion of oral epic, urged the found-
ing of a new, "non-Aristotelian" criticism of Homer. In
fact, what may be called for, as Richard Janko has argued,
is a more complete appreciation of the old poetics.[8]

What we need is not to produce our own new basis
for reading Homer, but to recover as much as possible
what an ancient "reading" might have been based on; or
rather we might say that to gain greater access to what
Homer's audience heard in the epics—that is, to return
to the *oldest* way of hearing Homer—would be, paradox-
ically, to achieve for ourselves new grounds for interpreting the *Iliad* and *Odyssey*. Just as basic etymological
studies of single words (using modern tools of linguistic
reconstruction) have brought us closer to the meaning
of traditional diction, and finally of Homeric themes,[9]

8. J. A. Notopoulos, "Studies in Early Greek Poetry," *HSCP*
68 (1964): 1–77, esp. 54–65. See now the discussion in R. Janko,
The Iliad: A Commentary, Vol. IV: Books 13–16 (Cambridge,
1992), xi, for the most recent statement of his view.

9. In particular the exemplary studies by E. Benveniste, *Le
vocabulaire des institutions indo-européennes I, II* (Paris, 1969); also
R. Schmitt, *Dichtung und Dichtersprache in indogermanischer Zeit*
(Wiesbaden, 1967). See the notable contributions of D. Frame,
The Myth of Return in Early Greek Epic (New Haven, 1978); A. L.
Bergren, *The Etymology and Usage of* ΠΕΙΡΑΡ *in Early Greek Po-
etry,* American Classical Studies 2, American Philological Asso-
ciation (New York, 1975); as well as L. C. Muellner, *The Meaning
of Homeric* ΕΥΧΟΜΑΙ *through its Formulas* (Innsbruck, 1976);
F. Mawet, *Le vocabulaire homérique de la douleur* (Brussels, 1979);
Sacks, *Traditional Phrase in Homer;* and S. Edmunds, *Homeric
Nēpios* (New York, 1990), all of which develop a careful analysis
of semantic field and contextual restrictions to supplement etymological reconstruction.

similarly, by uncovering the constituent components of a single Iliadic character we may come closer to understanding how the *Iliad* conjoined these elements and what the Homeric audience recognized in the depiction of that character.

In our pursuit of the poetic archaeology of Homer, small fragments of evidence will prove indispensable. If careful excavation and comparative analysis of relevant testimony outside the *Iliad* can show us how to fit together disparate pieces of a mythopoeic entity like Thetis—as we proceed on the assumption that they were once intact, and recognizably so—then even a single successful linkage can show us where to look for further interlocking connections. It can help us to see the shape of the whole structure; it may even turn out to be a cornerstone.

The Epic Cycle has emerged as our most productive (if controversial) resource for understanding the "uniqueness of Homer." [10] The search for the sources of the *Iliad,* as it was pursued, with exceptional imagination and industry, by scholars in the middle decades of this century, focused attention on the lost poems of the Epic Cycle—whose contents are known to us only indirectly, in a summary dating to the second century A.D. [11]—

10. The phrase is J. Griffin's; see his article "The Epic Cycle and the Uniqueness of Homer," *JHS* 97 (1977): 39–53.

11. For the plot summaries of the Cycle poems contained in Proclus's *Chrestomathia,* and testimonia and fragments, see T. W. Allen, ed., *Hymns, Epic Cycle,* vol. 5 of *Homeri Opera* (Oxford, 1912), 93–143.

as the crucial clue to finding "das Homerische in Homer."[12] This goal remained elusive to those concerned with specifying the *Iliad*'s literary origins within the Cycle poems' sequence of narratives, as sketched by Proclus's summary, from the genesis of the Trojan War to its aftermath; but their scholarly investigations were stimulating in the scrutiny to which they subjected puzzling and obscure passages of the *Iliad*.[13] And although their efforts to reconstruct the *Iliad*'s specific literary prototypes were inconclusive, their discussions of the common features shared by the *Iliad* and the Cycle poems were fruitful, because in attempting to establish which work constituted model and which transformation or revision the "neoanalyst" approach gave impor-

12. Georg Schoeck, Ilias *und* Aethiopis: *Kyklische Motive in homerischer Brechung* (Zurich, 1961), 10.

13. In fact, the "neoanalyst" approach could have been indispensable in sidestepping debates that equated originality with pure invention, had it not been concerned with pinning down specific textual prototypes for the *Iliad*. The principal exponents of "neoanalysis" include H. Pestalozzi, *Die* Achilleis *als Quelle der* Ilias (Erlenbach-Zurich, 1945); W. Kullmann, *Die Quellen der* Ilias, Hermes Einzelschriften 14 (Wiesbaden, 1960); W. Schadewaldt, *Von Homers Welt und Werk,* 2d ed. (Stuttgart, 1952), 155ff.; as well as Kakridis, *Homeric Researches;* and Schoeck, Ilias *und* Aethiopis. A discussion of some of the results of the neoanalytic method is contained in K. Reinhardt, *Die* Ilias *und ihr Dichter* (Göttingen, 1961), 349ff. For recent expositions of the approach as a whole, see A. Heubeck, *Die homerische Frage* (Darmstadt, 1974; reprint, 1988), 40ff.; and W. Kullmann, "Zur Methode der Neoanalyse in der Homerforschung," *Wiener Studien* n.s. 15 (1981): 5–42; a critical assessment is offered by A. Dihle, *Homer-Probleme* (Opladen, 1970); see esp. pp. 19–44 in the latter.

tant consideration to the general question of the *Iliad*'s adaptation of preexisting traditional material, such as that inherited by the Cycle poems and (despite their later date) embedded in them.[14]

Especially illuminating along these lines was the work of J. Th. Kakridis, whose studies in the morphology and transformation of story patterns are grounded in solid ethnographic empiricism.[15] Subsequent researches showed in detail that the Cycle poems inherit traditions contingent to our *Iliad* and *Odyssey* and preserve story patterns, motifs, and type-scenes that are as archaic as the material in the Homeric poems, to which they are related collaterally, rather than by descent.[16] The Cycle poems and the *Iliad* offer invaluable mutual perspective on the recombination of elements deriving from a com-

14. A. Severyns, *Le cycle épique dans l'école d'Aristarque* (Liège, 1928), 313, dates the *Aethiopis* to the eighth century, but even an appoximate dating for the Cycle cannot be secure. See Nagy, *Best of the Achaeans,* 42–43. The Cycle exhibits linguistic and stylistic features that indicate that it is in certain respects less developed, or more primitive, than the *Iliad* and *Odyssey* (the *enthen* phenomenon, for example); similarly, the composition of the Cycle poems was not monumental (so the interlocking of their stories suggests). On these features, see the useful contribution of Notopoulos, "Early Greek Oral Poetry," esp. 27–41, which demonstrates the orality of the Cycle poems and arrives independently at the same conclusions as Kakridis, *Homeric Researches,* esp. 90. See as well the discussion in C. H. Whitman, *Homer and the Heroic Tradition* (Cambridge, Mass., 1958), 181–82.

15. See note 6 above.

16. Most important is the early research of Bernard Fenik; see especially his Iliad X *and the* Rhesus: *The Myth* (Brussels, 1964) and *Typical Battle Scenes;* also Kullman, *Quellen der* Ilias.

mon source in myth, which makes possible the continuous evolution of themes and characters appropriate to
individual epic treatments—a dynamic process that must
be understood as a function not only of the individual
genius of a given practitioner of oral poetry, but of the
"many centuries of what must have been the most re-
fined sort of elite performer/audience interaction,"[17]
through which the focus and central concerns of poetic
entities like the *Iliad* and the *Odyssey* could develop, reflecting the developing consciousness of their culture.

Similarly, as we shall see, an important source of
comparative evidence offering insight into the themes of
the *Iliad* is choral lyric poetry, where treatment of closely
related mythic material provides the possibility of re-
covering archaic poetic traditions not overtly employed
by Homer.[18] As Emile Benveniste has demonstrated,
we may even see preserved in Pindar poetic traditions
whose Indo-European provenance is clearly discernible.[19] On a similar basis, evidence from Hesiodic poetry
proves indispensable.[20]

17. Nagy, *Best of the Achaeans,* 79. For a discussion of the relationship between the *Iliad* and the Cycle poems in the realm of
character development, see Whitman, *Homer and the Heroic Tradition,* 154–80.

18. See the discussion of traces of the *kourotrophos,* as confirmed by Pindar, in Sinos, *Meaning of* Philos.

19. See Benveniste's discussion of *Pythian* 3.40–55 in "La doctrine médicale des Indo-Européens," *RHR* 130 (1945): 5–12.

20. See G. P. Edwards, *The Language of Hesiod in Its Traditional Context* (Oxford, 1971); and H. Koller, "Das kitharodische

Because the contents of myth must necessarily be adapted to the restrictions and demands of poetic form, such apparently disparate evidence can shed valuable light on the criteria involved in heroic epic's generic regulation of its content. It may illuminate, moreover, any given epic's idiosyncratic handling of content, beyond the first level of adaptation to the formal conventions of epic, to convey the particular ideas and themes of a particular composition—a process that comparison with epic other than the *Iliad* also shows us. It is essential to bear in mind these two operative levels of selection in order to escape the automatic conclusion that traditional material that does not have an overt role in the *Iliad* was "not known" to Homer, and, rather, to perceive that either the genre did not encompass it or the thematic development of a particular epic composition did not appropriate it as directly functional. From the latter perspective, as we shall see, the *Aethiopis* is especially interesting for the student of the *Iliad,* featuring as it does an alternative development of the theme of the hero's acquisition of immortality through his mother.

Thus, as noted above, the *Iliad* all but ignores that not inconsequential piece of Iliadic prehistory, the Judgment of Paris; and yet, as we discover in Book 24—although not until then—the Judgment of Paris is indeed known to Homer, but carefully contained in a brief reference.

Prooimion: Eine formgeschichtliche Untersuchung," *Philologus* 100 (1956): 159–206.

Similarly, we may note that neither the *Iliad* nor the *Odyssey* overtly includes or elaborates theogonic mythology, although the myth of the struggle for divine sovereignty is a fundamental and pervasive one.[21] But the poems' references to "Zeus, son of Kronos" (as well as to other divine relations) make clear that the *Iliad* and the *Odyssey* assume a divine order dependent upon the myth of succession in heaven. We owe our familiarity with the content of that myth to Hesiod's *Theogony;* without it we would be unaware of the developed "history" of the Olympians implicit in the *Iliad*'s use of Zeus's patronymic.[22] Comparably, it has been shown that the reference to the wall built by the Achaeans in *Iliad* 12 evokes a complex myth of destruction to which even the myth of the Flood has been assimilated; yet we would have no awareness of such a myth without the *Cypria* and the Hesiodic Catalogue, as well as comparative evidence from the Near East.[23] In such instances, without a knowledge of mythological material from outside the *Iliad* and the *Odyssey,* not only would we not be able to identify what lies behind the allusions, but we would not even recognize that they are allusions.

21. See S. Littleton, "The Kingship in Heaven Theme," in *Myth and Law among the Indo-Europeans,* ed. J. Puhvel (Berkeley, 1970), 83–121, esp. 85–93.

22. See L. M. Slatkin "Genre and Generation in the *Odyssey,*" ΜΗΤΙΣ 1, no. 2 (1986): 259–68.

23. See R. Scodel, "The Achaean Wall and the Myth of Destruction," *HSCP* 86 (1982): 33–50. For further discussion, see chapter 4 in this book.

For a clearer understanding of Homeric poetics we need to see that the exclusion of such traditional mythological material, or its displacement into more or less oblique references (rather than overt exposition), including its subordination within digressions, is a defining principle by which the *Iliad* demarcates its subject and orients the audience toward its treatment of its themes. Consider the vivid example of this illustrated by the observation known as Monro's Law, so called after the editor who formulated it in his 1901 edition of the *Odyssey:* that the *Odyssey* "never repeats or refers to any incident related in the *Iliad.*"[24] It is scarcely possible to imagine that the *Odyssey* was composed without the slightest knowledge of the *Iliad* and its tradition, given its reliance throughout on the Trojan story for its own background.[25] It is certainly more likely that this "exclusion" of the *Iliad* is part of a deliberate narrative strategy that serves the *Odyssey*'s goal of staking out its own poetic territory in relation to the *Iliad,* according to its own bearings.

It is a reasonable surmise, then, that numerous allusions to traditional material may go unidentified by the modern reader unless special effort is made to locate them. If we make the effort, we will be able to discern

24. D. B. Monro, ed., *Homer's* Odyssey, vol. 2, books 13–24 (Oxford, 1901), 325.

25. D. L. Page imagined this, however. See *The Homeric Odyssey* (Oxford, 1955), 158. For a perspective that refutes Page's argument, see Nagy, *Best of the Achaeans,* chap. 1, esp. 20ff.

both foreground and background in the poems' use of mythology and gain a clearer picture of how that mythology is integrated or subsumed. In this way, we will be able to avoid not only denying to Homer knowledge that we did not realize he possessed, but also—and just as importantly—ascribing to him supposed "inventions" that are in fact part of a received heritage and have been employed to be recognized as such. Thus we may achieve a fuller sense of how the epics' specific relation to tradition informs their self-definition.

1

The Helplessness of Thetis

In a key passage in Book 1 of the *Iliad* Achilles, in order to obtain from Zeus the favor that will determine the trajectory of the plot, invokes not Athena or Hera, those powerful, inveterate pro-Greeks, but his mother. The *Iliad*'s presentation of Thetis, as we recall, is of a subsidiary deity who is characterized by helplessness and by impotent grief. Her presentation of herself is as the epitome of sorrow and vulnerability in the face of her son's mortality. Consider her lament to her Nereid sisters at 18.54–62.

ὤ μοι ἐγὼ δειλή, ὤ μοι δυσαριστοτόκεια,
ἥ τ' ἐπεὶ ἄρ τέκον υἱὸν ἀμύμονά τε κρατερόν τε,
ἔξοχον ἡρώων· ὁ δ' ἀνέδραμεν ἔρνεϊ ἶσος·
τὸν μὲν ἐγὼ θρέψασα, φυτὸν ὡς γουνῷ ἀλωῆς,
νηυσὶν ἐπιπροέηκα κορωνίσιν Ἴλιον εἴσω
Τρωσὶ μαχησόμενον· τὸν δ' οὐχ ὑποδέξομαι αὖτις
οἴκαδε νοστήσαντα δόμον Πηλήϊον εἴσω.
ὄφρα δέ μοι ζώει καὶ ὁρᾷ φάος ἠελίοιο
ἄχνυται, οὐδέ τί οἱ δύναμαι χραισμῆσαι ἰοῦσα.

Alas for my sorrow, alas for my wretched-best-
        childbearing,
since I bore a child faultless and powerful,
preeminent among heroes; and he grew like a young
        shoot,
I nourished him like a tree on an orchard's slope,
I sent him forth with the curved ships to Ilion
to fight the Trojans. But never again shall I
        welcome him
returning home to the house of Peleus.
Still, while he lives and looks on the sunlight
he grieves, and I, going to him, am all unable to
        help him.

We can hardly fail to question, then, why a figure of evidently minor stature—whose appearances in the poem are few—serves such a crucial function in its plot. Why, that is, does the poem assign to Thetis the awesome role of persuading Zeus to set in motion the events of the *Iliad,* to invert the inevitable course of the fall of Troy? Our initial answer to this might be, because Achilles is her son, and this poem is his story; but a methodologically more fruitful way of posing the question is, why has the *Iliad* taken as its hero the son of Thetis?

Let us begin by recalling the specific terms of Achilles' appeal to his mother in Book 1. He asks Thetis to make his request of Zeus, reminding her of how she saved Zeus when the other Olympians wished to bind him:

ἀλλὰ σύ, εἰ δύνασαί γε, περίσχεο παιδὸς ἐῆος·
ἐλθοῦσ' Οὔλυμπόνδε Δία λίσαι, εἴ ποτε δή τι
ἢ ἔπει ὤνησας κραδίην Διὸς ἠὲ καὶ ἔργῳ.

πολλάκι γάρ σεο πατρὸς ἐνὶ μεγάροισιν ἄκουσα
εὐχομένης, ὅτ᾽ ἔφησθα κελαινεφέϊ Κρονίωνι
οἴη ἐν ἀθανάτοισιν ἀεικέα λοιγὸν ἀμῦναι,
ὁππότε μιν ξυνδῆσαι Ὀλύμπιοι ἤθελον ἄλλοι,
Ἥρη τ᾽ ἠδὲ Ποσειδάων καὶ Παλλὰς Ἀθήνη·
ἀλλὰ σὺ τόν γ᾽ ἐλθοῦσα, θεά, ὑπελύσαο δεσμῶν,
ὦχ᾽ ἑκατόγχειρον καλέσασ᾽ ἐς μακρὸν Ὄλυμπον,
ὃν Βριάρεων καλέουσι θεοί, ἄνδρες δέ τε πάντες
Αἰγαίων᾽—ὁ γὰρ αὖτε βίην οὗ πατρὸς ἀμείνων—
ὅς ῥα παρὰ Κρονίωνι καθέζετο κύδεϊ γαίων·
τὸν καὶ ὑπέδεισαν μάκαρες θεοὶ οὐδ᾽ ἔτ᾽ ἔδησαν.
τῶν νῦν μιν μνήσασα παρέζεο καὶ λαβὲ γούνων,
αἴ κέν πως ἐθέλῃσιν ἐπὶ Τρώεσσιν ἀρῆξαι,
τοὺς δὲ κατὰ πρύμνας τε καὶ ἀμφ᾽ ἅλα ἔλσαι
   Ἀχαιοὺς
κτεινομένους, ἵνα πάντες ἐπαύρωνται βασιλῆος,
γνῷ δὲ καὶ Ἀτρεΐδης εὐρὺ κρείων Ἀγαμέμνων
ἣν ἄτην, ὅ τ᾽ ἄριστον Ἀχαιῶν οὐδὲν ἔτεισεν.

(1.393–412)

But you, if you are able to, protect your own son:
going to Olympos, pray to Zeus, if in fact you ever
aided the heart of Zeus by word or action.
For I have often heard you in my father's halls
avowing it, when you declared that from Kronos'
   son of the dark clouds
you alone among the immortals warded off
   unseemly destruction
at the time when the other Olympians wanted to
   bind him,
Hera and Poseidon and Pallas Athena;
but you went, goddess, and set him free from his
   bonds,

quickly summoning the hundred-handed one to
    high Olympos,
the one whom the gods call Briareos, but all men
    call
Aigaion—for he is greater in strength than his
    father—
who, rejoicing in his glory, sat beside the son of
    Kronos.
And the blessed gods feared him, and ceased
    binding Zeus.
Reminding him of these things now sit beside him
    and take his knees,
in the hope that he may somehow be willing to help
    the Trojans
and the others—the Achaeans—to force against the
    ships' sterns and around the sea
as they are slaughtered, so that they may all benefit
    from their king,
and so that the son of Atreus, wide-ruling
    Agamemnon, may realize
his disastrous folly, that he did not honor the best of
    the Achaeans.

Here we see the *Iliad* alluding to aspects of Thetis's
mythology that it does not elaborate and that do not
overtly reflect the subject matter of heroic poetry. Why
does it do so? The question is twofold: why does it allude to Thetis's power, and why does its reference remain only an allusion? Why does it, moreover, present
us with an apparent contradiction: if the mother of
Achilles is so helpless, why was she able to rescue Zeus;
and if she rescued Zeus, why is she now so helpless?

Why does the *Iliad* remind us of Thetis's efficacious power in another context while it presents her to us in an attitude of lamentation and grief without recourse?

In order to establish the proper framework for answering these questions, we begin our poetic archaeology. If we can set the Homeric use of Thetis into the perspective of her mythology, we may be led, as suggested earlier, to a deeper comprehension of Homeric poetics as well as to a richer appreciation of the specific themes associated with Achilles' divine origin. Our best initial index of comparison with the *Iliad*'s Thetis is afforded by Thetis's role in another epic treatment, the Cycle's *Aethiopis*, where we are presented not only with Thetis and Achilles but with a strikingly similar relationship, namely that of the divine Dawn Eos and her son Memnon.

The heroic identity of the Trojan ally Memnon was established in the *Aethiopis*, whose now-lost five books related his single combat against Achilles, among other events.[1] In the *Aethiopis*, the confrontation between Achilles and Memnon seems to have made use of the same narrative features that characterize the climactic duel of *Iliad* 22: the contest followed upon the death of Achilles' close friend at the hands of his chief Trojan ad-

---

1. See Proclus's summary in Allen, *Homeri opera,* vol. 5, 106. For a discussion of the range of its contents, see Severyns, *Cycle épique,* 313–27; also G. L. Huxley, *Greek Epic Poetry: From Eumelos to Panyassis* (London, 1969), 144–49. On the structure and style of the Cycle, see Kullmann, *Quellen der* Ilias, 204ff., esp. 212–14.

versary and was preceded by Thetis's prophecy of the outcome.

In the *Aethiopis* Achilles avenged the killing of Nestor's son Antilokhos, whose death at the hands of Memnon is referred to at *Odyssey* 4.187–88. Proclus's summary of this section goes as follows:

Μέμνων δὲ ὁ Ἠοῦς υἱὸς ἔχων ἠφαιστότευκτον πανοπλίαν παραγίνεται τοῖς Τρωσὶ βοηθήσων· καὶ Θέτις τῷ παιδὶ τὰ κατὰ τὸν Μέμνονα προλέγει. καὶ συμβολῆς γενομένης Ἀντίλοχος ὑπὸ Μέμνονος ἀναιρεῖται, ἔπειτα Ἀχιλλεὺς Μέμνονα κτείνει· καὶ τούτῳ μὲν Ἠὼς παρὰ Διὸς αἰτησαμένη ἀθανα- σίαν δίδωσι.[2]

So Memnon, the son of Eos, wearing armor made by Hephaistos, arrives to aid the Trojans; and Thetis prophesies to her son things about Memnon. In the encounter that takes place Antilokhos is killed by Memnon, whereupon Achilles kills Memnon. Then Eos, having asked Zeus for immortality for Memnon, bestows it on him.

Memnon, although functioning in a role like Hector's, is a mirror image of the Iliadic Achilles. The association of these two heroes, not principally as adversaries but as parallel figures, is reflected in the poetry of Pindar, who more than once describes Memnon in terms appropriate to Achilles in the *Iliad*—singularly so, as they are the terms Achilles uses of himself—calling him Μέμνονος οὐκ ἀπονοστήσαντος ("Memnon who did

2. See Allen, *Homeri Opera*, vol. 5, 106.

not return home again").[3] Preeminent among his allies, bearing armor made by Hephaistos, Memnon is the child of a divine mother, Eos, and a mortal father, Tithonos. This last feature was apparently given emphasis by the narrative shape of the *Aethiopis:* the actual presence of the two goddesses Eos and Thetis on the field of battle, contrasting the mortal vulnerability of the opponents with their equal heritage from the mother's immortal line, may have generated the poem's narrative tension.[4] What the *Iliad* treats as a unique and isolating phenomenon, the *Aethiopis* developed along alternative traditional lines, giving prominence to the theme of mortal-immortal duality by doubling its embodiment, in the two heroes Memnon and Achilles.

Iconographic evidence supplements the version of the myth given by the *Aethiopis.* The symmetry of the two heroes is reflected in numerous examples of archaic pictorial art.[5] Vase paintings illustrating the *monomachia*

3. *Nem.* 6.50. See also *Ol.* 2.83 and *Nem.* 3.63. References are to the Oxford edition of Pindar by C. M. Bowra (1947; reprint, 1961).

4. To precisely what effect the *Aethiopis* used this traditional parallelism is of course a matter for speculation; in any case, as the iconographic evidence indicates (see note 6 below), the poem very likely transmitted this inherited confrontation without special innovation. W. Burkert, *Greek Religion* (Cambridge, Mass., 1985), 121, observes, "When Achilles fights with Memnon, the two divine mothers, Thetis and Eos, rush to the scene—this was probably the subject of a pre-Iliad epic song."

5. Pausanias (3.18.12) reports that their confrontation in single combat was depicted on the decorated throne in the sanctuary at Amyklae in Laconia. See the discussion in A. Schneider, *Der*

of Memnon and Achilles significantly portray Eos and
Thetis facing each other, each at her son's side.[6] The
parallelism persists even in the outcome of the duel, although ultimately one hero will win and the other will
lose. Vase painting corroborates the existence, in the
tradition also shared by the *Aethiopis,* of a *kērostasia* in
which Hermes weighs the *kēres* of Memnon and Achilles in the presence of Eos and Thetis.[7] In the *Aethiopis,*

---

troische Sagenkreis in der ältesten griechischen Kunst (Leipzig, 1886),
143ff; also Pestalozzi, Achilleis *als Quelle der* Ilias, 11.

6. In his important study *The* Iliad *in Early Greek Art* (Copenhagen, 1967), K. Friis Johansen, referring to "a well-known type
of picture that was very popular in early Greek art, a conventional
monomachy framed by two standing female figures," points out
that "there can be no doubt that this type was originally invented
for the fight between Achilles and Memnon in the presence of
their mothers Thetis and Eos" (200–201). According to Pausanias
(5.19.2), the scene was also represented on the relief-decorated
chest of Kypselos at Olympia: the two heroes duel, each with his
mother at his side. M. E. Clark and W. D. E. Coulson discuss the
iconography of the *Aethiopis* and its adaptations in painting, as
well as the poem's relation to the *Iliad,* in "Memnon and Sarpedon," *MH* 35 (1978): 65–73. See also K. Schefold, *Myth and
Legend in Early Greek Art* (London, 1966), 45, together with plate
10 (Athens National Museum 3961.911).

7. On the iconography of this subject, see *RE* 23.2 (1959),
1442, s.v. "Psychostasie" (E. Wust); G. E. Lung, "Memnon:
Archäologische Studien zur *Aethiopis*" (Diss., Bonn, 1912),
14–19; and the discussion in Johansen, Iliad *in Early Greek Art,*
261. The weighing of the fates of Memnon and Achilles is not
specifically mentioned by Proclus in his summary, although it
provided the subject for Aeschylus's lost play *Psychostasia,* as we
learn from schol. A ad 8.70 and Eust. 8. 73.699.31, among others.
For views in support of its existence in the *Aethiopis,* see Clark
and Coulson, "Memnon and Sarpedon"; B. C. Dietrich, "The
Judgment of Zeus," *RhM* 107 (1964): 97–125, esp. 112–14; Severyns, *Cycle épique,* 318–19.

the paired mothers are equated in their involvement in the struggle, each present to protect her son.

The efforts of Thetis and Eos in the *Aethiopis* are essentially identical. In only one respect are Thetis and Eos distinguished in Proclus's summary of the *Aethiopis*. Unlike Eos, Thetis communicates to Achilles some foreknowledge about his adversary: τὰ κατὰ τὸν Μέμνονα προλέγει ("Thetis prophesies to her son about Memnon"). In the reconstruction of the "Memnonis" proposed by neoanalytic studies, Thetis here foretells Achilles' imminent death, which is to follow upon his slaying of Memnon. According to this hypothesis, Thetis's prophetic warning here is the cause of Achilles' abstention from battle, which he will reenter only after the death of his friend Antilokhos.[8] This cannot be a conclusive reading, of course; nevertheless, we can appreciate what prompted it: the certain existence of a scene in the *Aethiopis* in which, at the very least, Thetis intervened with her divine foresight and maternal solicitude on behalf of her son's safety.

Eos requests of Zeus, and obtains, immortality for Memnon. Thetis does not actually ask Zeus for immortality for Achilles; but she herself "having snatched her

---

8. Schoeck, Ilias *und* Aethiopis, 38–48, contributes the interesting observation that the *Iliad* makes reference to a prophecy from Thetis precisely at those junctures where the question of Achilles' return to battle arises, e.g., 11.790ff.; 16.36–50. He argues that the *Iliad* in this way adverts to a "Memnonis" prototype, in which Thetis's prophecy was the specific cause of Achilles' absence from battle; that is, Achilles absented himself from battle at his mother's request.

son away from the pyre, transports him to the White
Island."[9] Like Elysion, the White Island represents the
refuge of immortality for heroes, where they live on
once they have not avoided but—even better—tran-
scended death.[10] The *Aethiopis,* then, emphasized the
hero's divine heritage as a way of separating him from
ordinary human existence and his access to communication with the gods as a way of resolving the conflict between heroic stature and mortal limitation.

The tradition represented by the *Aethiopis* and by our
iconographic examples thus posits an identity not only
between Achilles and Memnon but between Thetis and
Eos, based on their roles as immortal guardians and
protectors of their mortal children. From a narrative
standpoint this parallelism is more than an instance of
the Cycle's fondness for repetition or doublets.[11] The

9. See Allen, *Homeri opera,* vol. 5, 106.
10. The use of the White Island motif, like that of Elysion at
Odyssey 4.563, is an acknowledgment of the religious and social
phenomenon of the hero-cult, which is generally excluded from
direct reference in epic. E. Rohde, *Psyche: Seelencult und Unsterblichkeitsglaube der Griechen,* vol. 2, 4th ed. (Freiburg, 1898; Tübingen, 1907), 371, calls Leuke a "Sonderelysion" for Achilles. Rohde
offers a discussion of the thematic equivalence of Leuke, Elysion,
and the Isles of the Blessed on pp. 365–78. On Elysion as a cult
concept, see W. Burkert, "Elysion," *Glotta* 39 (1961): 208–13; and
Th. Hadzisteliou Price, "Hero-Cult and Homer," *Historia* 22
(1973): 133–34. On the traditional poetic diction of "snatching,"
or abducting, used (at least by Proclus) to describe Thetis's action
here, see note 28 below.
11. E. Howald examines doubling as a feature of the evolution
and transmission of myth in *Der Mythos als Dichtung* (Zurich,

Aethiopis shows us not a recapitulation of a prior situation by a subsequent one, but a rendering of the mythological equation between the two figures as a simultaneous juxtaposition, a mirroring, in which each reflects, and must assume the dimensions of, her counterpart.

The virtual identity of the two mothers asserted by the tradition transmitted by the *Aethiopis* as well as by pictorial representations reinforces the uniqueness of Thetis in the *Iliad,* the incomparable singularity of her position, to which the poem explicitly calls attention at 18.429–34:

Ἥφαιστ᾽, ἦ ἄρα δή τις, ὅσαι θεαί εἰσ᾽ ἐν Ὀλύμπῳ,
τοσσάδ᾽ ἐνὶ φρεσὶν ᾗσιν ἀνέσχετο κήδεα λυγρά,
ὅσσ᾽ ἐμοὶ ἐκ πασέων Κρονίδης Ζεὺς ἄλγε᾽ ἔδωκεν;
ἐκ μέν μ᾽ ἀλλάων ἁλιάων ἀνδρὶ δάμασσεν,
Αἰακίδῃ Πηλῆϊ, καὶ ἔτλην ἀνέρος εὐνὴν
πολλὰ μάλ᾽ οὐκ ἐθέλουσα.

Hephaistos, is there anyone, of all the goddesses on
    Olympos,
who has endured so many baneful sorrows in her
    heart,
as many as the griefs Zeus the son of Kronos has
    given me beyond all others?
Of all the daughters of the sea he forced on me a
    mortal man
Aiakos' son Peleus, and I endured the bed of a
    mortal man
Utterly unwilling though I was.

1937); on doublets in the Cycle in particular, see Howald's *Der Dichter der* Ilias (Erlenbach-Zurich, 1946), 125.

But if the *Iliad* treats Thetis's position as unparalleled, then an examination of its treatment in the light of the sources of the Thetis-Eos equation can serve as an introduction to the *Iliad*'s process of interpreting and selectively shaping its mythology, preserving for us aspects of Thetis that elucidate her role in the *Iliad* even when Eos is not present to help evoke them.

Comparative evidence indicates the connection of several female deities who are notable in Greek and Indic mythologies to the prototype of an Indo-European Dawn goddess, *Ausos.[12] The representatives of this important Indo-European figure who most closely assume her functions in their respective poetic traditions are Indic Uṣas and Greek Eos. The shared attributes of these Greek and Indic Dawn goddesses, which link them to their prototype, yield a still more productive legacy in Greek epic, however, where they are inherited by Aphrodite, among others.

In analyzing the elements that Aphrodite and Eos share and that identify them (with Uṣas) as descendants of the Indo-European Dawn goddess, we recognize motifs that are significant in the story of Thetis.[13] Chief

12. On the etymology of Attic Ἕως (= Ionic Ἠώς), see P. Chantraine, *Dictionnaire étymologique de la langue grecque* (Paris, 1968), 394–95.

13. The evidence for the Indo-European origins of Aphrodite, Eos, and Uṣas is presented in D. D. Boedeker, *Aphrodite's Entry into Greek Epic* (Leiden, 1974), whose subject is Greek epic's integration of Aphrodite's inherited features, through diction and theme, into its development of her character and role. See also the observations in P. Friedrich, *The Meaning of Aphrodite* (Chicago,

among these is the association of the immortal goddess with a mortal lover.[14] Like Uṣas in the Vedic hymns, Eos unites with various lovers, among whom Tithonos is prominent in epic; Aphrodite has union with several, notably Anchises; and Thetis is joined to Peleus. Although the outcome of a love relationship between immortal and mortal may be benign, the potential for extraordinary pathos in such a story is clear. In these instances the inherent tension resulting from the juxtaposition of immortal and mortal is involved with a specific and fundamental connection between the timeless goddesses and time itself.

The function of the Dawn goddess in Indo-European religious traditions, and hence the inherited function of Eos, is the model for this connection. Eos brings the day into being: in a sense she creates time, as at *Odyssey* 5.390:

ἀλλ' ὅτε δὴ τρίτον ἦμαρ ἐϋπλόκαμος τέλεσ' Ἠώς

but when beautiful-haired Dawn had accomplished
  the third day.

1978), who holds that "the Proto-Indo-European goddess of dawn was one of several main sources for the Greek Aphrodite" (31).

14. Boedeker, *Aphrodite's Entry,* 67, notes: "The tradition of the mortal lover of the Dawn-goddess is an old one; in Greek epic it is surely the most obvious aspect of Eos' mythology. Comparative evidence from the *Ṛg-Veda* indicates that this feature of solar mythology dates back to common Indo-European, although in Greek myth it may have been amplified beyond its original importance." See also C. P. Segal, "The Homeric Hymn to Aphrodite: A Structuralist Approach," *CW* 67 (1974): 205–12.

As she brings the day into existence and, in effect, controls time, time controls the lives of men, by aging them; yet the goddess herself is unaging, ever-renewed.[15] Eos's epithet ἠριγένεια (*ērigeneia*, "early-born") expresses the contrast between the consequences for men of her activity, and her own freedom from those consequences. From the human point of view, she is not simply immortal; she is the agent of the process by which the meaning of mortality is fulfilled.

Eos and her lovers serve as the model for goddess-mortal relationships, with their essential antithesis between the timelessness of the goddess and the temporality of her lover.[16] Eos and her lovers are even cited by characters *within* epic as exemplary of such relationships. Aphrodite herself tells Eos's story (*Hymn. Hom. Aphr.* 218–38); Kalypso knows it as well, even though, as the *Odyssey* points out, she lives very far away (*Od.* 5.121); and both compare it to their own stories. The marriage of Thetis to Peleus exhibits the same antithetical pattern. Because Eos typifies such goddess-mortal relationships, Thetis is perceived synchronically as being connected with her, as in the *Aethiopis,* and thus shares dictional features associated with her—although Thetis cannot definitively be shown, as Eos has been, to be a direct descendant, or hypostasis, of the Indo-European

15. On the similarly ambivalent nature of the Indic Dawn Uṣas, see A. K. Coomaraswamy, "The Darker Side of Dawn," *Smithsonian Miscellaneous Collections* 94.1 (1935): 1–18, esp. 4–6.

16. See Boedeker, *Aphrodite's Entry,* 69.

Dawn goddess; their relationship is structurally homolo-
gous, rather than historical.

In Greek epic, the themes attached to the goddess and
her mortal lover are recapitulated, with much greater
emphasis, in the relationship between the goddess and
her son, the offspring of her union with her mortal
lover. Eos and Memnon, as an instance of this, reinforce
the Eos-Thetis parallel. But in the case of Eos, the pattern of whose relationship with Tithonos is repeated in
part with Memnon—when she requests and obtains his
immortality—the erotic aspect of her mythology domi-
nates. Thetis's erotic aspect, discernible (as we shall see)
in the tradition followed by Pindar and Aeschylus, where
both mortal and immortal partners woo her, is subordinated to her maternal aspect, as she appears in the *Iliad*.

In the *Iliad,* the collocation of Thetis's activities with
early morning may reflect the association with Eos and
her time-related function, inherited from Indo-European
tradition. At 18.136, Thetis tells Achilles that she will
seek armor from Hephaistos for him at dawn: ἠῶθεν
γὰρ νεῦμαι ἅμ᾿ ἠελίῳ ἀνιόντι ("for I shall return at
dawn, with the sun's rising").[17] At 1.497, when Thetis
travels to Olympos to ask Zeus for the favor on behalf of Achilles, the adjective ἠερίη (*ēeriē*) is used to
describe her:

> ἥ γ᾿ ἀνεδύσετο κῦμα θαλάσσης,
> ἠερίη δ᾿ ἀνέβη μέγαν οὐρανὸν Οὔλυμπόν τε.
> (1.496–97)

17. This association is recalled by Apollonius (*Argon.* 4.841).

she rose from the sea's wave
and early in the morning ascended to the great sky
and Olympos.

Later, Hera rebukes Zeus for conferring with Thetis
at the latter's request, saying:

νῦν δ᾽ αἰνῶς δείδοικα κατὰ φρένα μή σε παρείπῃ
ἀργυρόπεζα Θέτις θυγάτηρ ἁλίοιο γέροντος·
ἠερίη γὰρ σοί γε παρέζετο καὶ λάβε γούνων.

(1.555–57)

But now I fear dreadfully that she won you over,
silver-footed Thetis, daughter of the old man of
        the sea,
for early in the morning she sat with you and
        clasped your knees.

Apart from being used of Thetis, ἠερίη occurs in
the *Iliad* only once (3.7). Like Eos's epithet ἠριγένεια
(*ērigeneia*, "early-born"), it may be related to ἦρι (*ēri*).[18]

18. See the discussion in Chantraine, *Dictionnaire étymologique,*
407. Chantraine observes that the usage of ἠέριος reflects alternative etymologies, both of which are susceptible to this morphology: *aer* and *awer*. These would yield separate meanings, either "early in the morning" or "mistlike." Both are appropriate
to Thetis. She does much of her traveling at dawn, but she also
rises from the sea ἠῦτ᾽ ὀμίχλη ("like a mist") at 1.359. In its epic
usage in association with Thetis, ἠερίη has the resonance of both
meanings, not as ambiguous but as surcharged with meaning: its
association with her conflates the two possibilities. Schoeck, *Ilias
und* Aethiopis, 41, comments, "Schon im Altertum war es strittig,
ob ἠερίη hier [1.497] 'in der Morgenfrühe' oder 'wie Luft' heisse.
Es ist denkbar, daß Homer selber mit den zwei Bedeutungen
spielt." On the connection of these motifs with Okeanos, see
Boedeker, *Aphrodite's Entry,* 69ff.

The use of ἠερίη and Thetis's early morning travels may evoke her ties to Ēōs ērigeneia and the connection of their power with time, the defining fact of human life.

The reason that such diction and the motifs to which it is attached have worked their way into the narrative is to be found in the themes of the epic as a whole.[19] A preeminent concern of our *Iliad* is the problem of mortality. While it is characteristic of epic not to confine its thematic expression to its principal character, the *Iliad* centers definitively in the monumental figure of Achilles, whose life represents the fullest embodiment of this theme.[20] In our *Iliad,* the mainspring of Achilles' developing sense of values is his consciousness of the

19. On the relationship between the words ἥρως ("hero") and ὥρα ("season, seasonality"), see W. Pötscher, "Hera und Heros," *RhM* 104 (1961): 302–55; on the association of the hero and ὥρα as a fundamental theme in Greek myth, see Sinos, *Meaning of Philos,* 13–26.

20. Just as the *Odyssey* is concerned with many variations on the theme of return to home and self—including the "homecomings" of Penelope, Agamemnon, Menelaos, Nestor, and Odysseus's companions—yet focuses on the *nostos* of Odysseus, so the *Iliad* presents numerous individual histories to illustrate the encompassing view expressed at 6.146–49:

οἵη περ φύλλων γενεή, τοίη δὲ καὶ ἀνδρῶν.
φύλλα τὰ μέν τ' ἄνεμος χαμάδις χέει, ἄλλα δέ θ' ὕλη
τηλεθόωσα φύει, ἔαρος δ' ἐπιγίγνεται ὥρη·
ὣς ἀνδρῶν γενεὴ ἡ μὲν φύει ἡ δ' ἀπολήγει.

As is the generation of leaves, so is that of men.
The wind showers the leaves to the ground,
but the budding wood blossoms, and the season of Spring arrives.
So one generation of men flourishes and the other fades away.

brevity of human life, and especially the extreme brevity
that the war enforces. He finds the meaning of any situation by measuring it against the irreducible fact of the
brevity of life. In the course of the poem, the value that
he assigns to such meaning will be transformed. Because his life will be short, his dishonor at the hands of
Agamemnon is initially seen to be all the more important; later, with Achilles' increased perspective on what
it means to have a short life, honor from Agamemnon
will have no value for him.

From the outset, the *Iliad* presents Achilles as pos-
sessing a powerful, personal sense of his own mortality.
His first assertion of this is to Thetis, when he originally
invokes her assistance at 1.352:

μῆτερ, ἐπεί μ᾿ ἔτεκές γε μινυνθάδιόν περ ἐόντα

Mother, since you did bear me to be short-lived.

That the adjective μινυνθάδιος (*minunthadios*, "short-
lived") is not just a neutral term for describing anyone
mortal but is highly charged and refers pointedly to
Achilles' own imminent death is evident from its other
occurrences in the poem. Elsewhere only Lykaon calls
himself *minunthadios* (21.84), when he is about to die
at Achilles' hands. At 15.612, Hektor is said to be "about
to be" *minunthadios,* which the subsequent lines make
explicit:[21]

21. Hektor and Lykaon are the two characters to whom Achilles expresses the necessity of recognizing and accepting death; as
he himself has done it, so they must do it as well. The adjective is

μινυνθάδιος γὰρ ἔμελλεν
ἔσσεσθ'· ἤδη γάρ οἱ ἐπόρνυε μόρσιμον ἦμαρ
Παλλὰς 'Αθηναίη ὑπὸ Πηλεΐδαο βίηφιν.
(15.612–14)

So Hektor was to be *minunthadios;*
for now Pallas Athena was already driving his death
day
upon him, beneath the strength of the son of Peleus.

Thetis's reply in Book 1 more than confirms the insight that ultimately, in Book 24, enables Achilles to
place his brief existence in the context of others' lives—
but through which, initially, he is isolated as epic poetry
isolates no other single hero. His role and his self-
perception converge, whereby the plot of the *Iliad* is
multiply determined. Thetis's response at 1.416,

ἐπεί νύ τοι αἶσα μίνυνθά περ, οὔ τι μάλα δήν

since now your destiny is brief, of no length,

uniquely then speaks of an αἶσα (*aisa*, "destiny, allot-
ment") that is brief, as though Achilles' *aisa*—his final
goal, that which is destined for him in the end—were
precisely identical with the process by which it is at-
tained. Elsewhere, *aisa* is either the literal end of life (as
at 24.428, 750) or it is the principle of destiny, the index
of whether one's actions are appropriate to one's nature.
A hero can act either *kata* or *huper aisan*—"according

used otherwise only of two Trojan warriors, Simoeisios and Hip-
pothoos, at the precise point at which each meets his death (4.478
= 17.302).

to" or "beyond, in contravention of" *aisa*—or he can have an evil *aisa*, but only Achilles has a *brief aisa*—a destiny that is nothing other than the span of his life.[22]

Equally remarkable is Thetis's use of the compound ὠκύμορος (*ōkumoros*), as her lament continues:

νῦν δ᾽ ἅμα τ᾽ ὠκύμορος καὶ ὀϊζυρὸς περὶ πάντων
ἔπλεο·

(1.417–18)

For now you are swift in fate and wretched beyond
all men.

Like *aisa*, the word *ōkumoros* acquires a new meaning when used of Achilles. Its principal meaning appears at 15.441, where Ajax uses it of the arrows belonging to the archer Teucer:

ποῦ νύ τοι ἰοὶ
ὠκύμοροι καὶ τόξον, ὅ τοι πόρε Φοῖβος Ἀπόλλων;
(15.440–41)

Where now are your arrows
of quick death and the bow that Phoibos Apollo
gave you?

Here the original meaning, "bringing swift death," is evident.[23] But elsewhere in the poem this adjective is applied only to Achilles and only by Thetis, who repeats it

22. See page 104.
23. This meaning is confirmed by the *Odyssey*'s use of the adjective at 22.75, where it is used of the arrows aimed against the suitors by Odysseus.

at 18.95, replying or prophesying in response to Achilles' declaration to avenge Patroklos's death:

> ὠκύμορος δή μοι, τέκος, ἔσσεαι, οἳ' ἀγορεύεις·

> Then you will be swift in fate, my child, from what
> you say.

Later in Book 18, requesting the aid of Hephaistos, she says:

> αἴ κ' ἐθέλῃσθα
> υἱεῖ ἐμῷ ὠκυμόρῳ δόμεν ἀσπίδα
> (18.457–58)

> if you are willing to give a shield to my son swift
> in fate.

Used of Achilles, the word describes not the agent but the victim of *moros*. In effect both functions are joined in Achilles, who participates in bringing about his own swift death. Because *moros* can mean destiny as well as death, *ōkumoros* characterizing Achilles could be said to mean "swiftly fated" and to denote the same idea expressed by *aisa minuntha,* namely, that for Achilles destiny is a synonym for life span.

Achilles, then, has special diction that distinguishes his experience as the limiting case of the experience of mortality. Its use by Thetis lays great stress on this; it is the essence of her appeal to Zeus:

> τίμησόν μοι υἱόν, ὃς ὠκυμορώτατος ἄλλων
> ἔπλετ'·
> (1.505–6)

> Honor my son who is swiftest in death of all
> mortals.

The poem uses Thetis to view Achilles' life from a cosmic perspective that enhances its stature as it throws into relief its brevity. Her close connection with Achilles' recognition of his mortal condition—and with all the most human aspects of his nature—contrasts sharply with the role shared by Eos and Thetis in the *Aethiopis*, which emphasized their sons' access to divinity. It shows as well how Achilles has been developed in the *Iliad* beyond the stage in which he and Memnon were correspondingly parallel and minimally differentiated from each other.

The *Iliad* establishes Achilles as the limiting case of human brevity and thus insists on the disparity between his situation and the timelessness of Thetis.[24] Unlike the *Aethiopis*, however, the *Iliad* does so not in order to value more highly the acquisition of immortality, but to define the boundaries of human life that it accepts as final. Thetis and her mythology are put to radically different use in the *Iliad*. Through her the *Iliad* offers not the immortality of the *Aethiopis*, but a conception of heroic stature as inseparable from human limitation and of

---

24. At 17.446ff. Zeus pities the horses of Peleus because although immortal they are yoked to the lives of men who, being mortal, are especially given over to suffering (ὀϊζυρώτεροι). But it is Achilles who has been called ὠκύμορος καὶ ὀϊζυρὸς περὶ πάντων, at 1.417; so that what mortals are by nature, Achilles is *most*.

heroic experience as a metaphor for the condition of mortality, with all its contradictions. No hero in the *Iliad* is given immortality, which would be utterly incompatible with such a perspective; the possibility is entirely absent. The premise of the poem, as conveyed through the characters' own perceptions, is that the idea of immortality expresses only the extreme of imagination against which the reality of human potential and limitation is measured and comprehended.[25]

Achilles' discovery of identity—of values, of morality—is inseparable from the apprehension of mortality; that discovery becomes necessary and has meaning only if immortality is precluded. The battle as a context for events to be celebrated in epic may well have originated as a setting for descriptions of extraordinary exploits involving physical prowess and designating a hierarchy of heroes. But where the life-and-death import of the action may in other epic treatments have been only a framework, in the *Iliad* it becomes the subject itself. The heroism of Achilles emerges not so much because his exploits distinguish him as because the battle serves as a setting in which every choice, every action, becomes all-important—an arena where one's life is most closely bound to the lives of others and where, for that rea-

25. As expressed, for instance, in the famous speech of Sarpedon to Glaukos at 12.309–28. On this subject, see the penetrating discussion of Whitman, *Homer and the Heroic Tradition*, 181–220; see as well the insights in S. L. Schein, *The Mortal Hero: An Introduction to Homer's* Iliad (Berkeley, 1984), 67–84.

son, the definition of the self comes urgently into question. Prowess becomes peripheral to the crisis of the self relative to one's own expectations and the lives of others.

To speak of the evolution of the *Iliad*, therefore, is to speak of the growth of the idea of the hero. The very story the poem tells embodies that evolution, describing the coming into being of the new hero. It tells the story of the making of its own subject matter. This is what Thetis's request to Zeus in *Iliad* 1 signifies, in contrast to Eos's in the *Aethiopis*. For in this sense, what Thetis asks Zeus to give Achilles is the opportunity to become the hero of the *Iliad*, to create the terms by which heroism will be redefined.

The *Iliad* explores the theme of mortality precisely by evoking and transforming an important traditional motif in such a way that the transformation expresses the premise of the poem. Placed in the context of the tradition the *Iliad* evokes, the equation of Thetis and Eos seeking immortality for their sons, Thetis's appeals to Zeus and later to Hephaistos on behalf of Achilles' vulnerability can be understood as significant examples of how the poem develops its major theme.

Certain elements in the constellation of motifs common to the divinities sharing the mythology of the Dawn goddess are preserved by the *Iliad;* others are significantly reworked. The motif of the goddess's protection of the mortal hero she loves is a central traditional feature shared by the immortal mothers (and lovers) who inherit, or are assimilated to, the mythology of the

Dawn goddess.[26] Its variations, apart from Eos and Thetis in the *Aethiopis,* include Kalypso in the *Odyssey* and Aphrodite in the *Homeric Hymn to Aphrodite* as well as in the *Iliad.*[27] This tradition is well known to the *Iliad,* where in two dramatic episodes Aphrodite acts to protect her favorites from imminent danger, snatching them away from battle at the crucial moment. In Book 3 she rescues Paris as he is about to be overpowered by Menelaos:

τὸν δ' ἐξήρπαξ' Ἀφροδίτη
ῥεῖα μάλ' ὥς τε θεός, ἐκάλυψε δ' ἄρ' ἠέρι πολλῇ,
κὰδ δ' εἷσ' ἐν θαλάμῳ εὐώδεϊ κηώεντι.

(3.380–82)

But Aphrodite snatched him up
easily as a god may, and enclosed him in a dense mist
and put him down in his fragrant bedchamber.

26. Sinos, *Meaning of* Philos, has shown in detail that the *kourotrophos* or nurturing function of the goddess, revealed in the diction of vegetal growth, as, for example, at *Iliad* 18.437–38, is apparent in the relationship in cult between the *kourotrophos* goddess and the *kouros.* The protection motif is a correlate of this function in myth. See also R. Merkelbach, "ΚΟΡΟΣ," *ZPE* 8 (1971): 80; and P. Vidal-Naquet, "Le chasseur noir et l'origine de l'éphébie athénienne," *Économies-sociétés-civilisations* 23 (1968): 947–49.

27. On the related attributes of these goddesses, see Boedeker, *Aphrodite's Entry,* 64–84. Apart from the Dawn goddess hypostases, Demeter in the *Homeric Hymn to Demeter* appears in the role of *kourotrophos* to Demophon; see the commentary ad 231–55 (esp. 237ff. with remarks on Achilles and Thetis) in N. J. Richardson, ed., *The Homeric Hymn to Demeter* (Oxford, 1974; reprint, 1979), 231ff.

In Book 5 it is Aeneas whom she saves, from the on-slaught of Diomedes:

> ἀμφὶ δ᾽ ἐὸν φίλον υἱὸν ἐχεύατο πήχεε λευκώ,
> πρόσθε δέ οἱ πέπλοιο φαεινοῦ πτύγμ᾽ ἐκάλυψεν,
> ἕρκος ἔμεν βελέων, μή τις Δαναῶν ταχυπώλων
> χαλκὸν ἐνὶ στήθεσσι βαλὼν ἐκ θυμὸν ἕλοιτο.
> Ἡ μὲν ἐὸν φίλον υἱὸν ὑπεξέφερεν πολέμοιο·
>
> (5.314–18)

and around her dear son she threw her white arms,
and in front of him she wrapped a fold of her
   shining robe,
to be a shield against weapons, lest any of the
   Danaans with quick horses
should take his life from him, striking bronze into
   his chest.
So she bore her dear son away from the battle.

To snatch a hero from danger, to protect him from death, however, offers a paradox of which the *Iliad* and *Odyssey* are conscious: that preserving a hero from death means denying him a heroic life.[28] Thus Kalypso, who compares her intention toward Odysseus with Eos's abduction of Orion,[29] wants by sequestering Odysseus to

28. For an analysis of the structure and diction of similar episodes of abduction and "preservation," especially the ambivalence inherent in such episodes' use of the particular terminology of snatching, kidnapping, and concealing, see Nagy, *Greek Mythology and Poetics,* 223–62, esp. 242–57. This same terminology (as transmitted by Proclus, at any rate) is used to designate Thetis's action in the *Aethiopis* in snatching Achilles from the pyre (N.B. the use of *anarpasasa*), after which she "preserves" him on the White Island.

29. *Od.* 5.121–24.

offer him immortality; but this would inevitably mean the loss of his goal, the impossibility of completing the travels, the denial of his identity. From a perspective that is as intrinsic to the *Odyssey* as to the *Iliad,* it would mean the extinction of heroic subject matter, the negation of epic. Kalypso, "the concealer," uses persuasive arguments in her attempt to hide Odysseus from mortality. Her ultimate failure measures the hero's commitment to his mortal existence—not, as she believes, the Olympian gods' jealousy, but their participation in human values.

Aphrodite, on the other hand, is a successful concealer, shielding her favorites by hiding them, Paris in the cloud of mist and Aeneas in her flowing robe.[30] She enters the battle swiftly at the critical moment to save the life of her son, or, in the case of Paris, her protégé:

Καί νύ κεν ἔνθ᾽ ἀπόλοιτο ἄναξ ἀνδρῶν Αἰνείας,
εἰ μὴ ἄρ᾽ ὀξὺ νόησε Διὸς θυγάτηρ Ἀφροδίτη,
μήτηρ, ἥ μιν ὑπ᾽ Ἀγχίσῃ τέκε βουκολέοντι·
(5.311–13)

And now Aeneas lord of men would have perished
    there
if the daughter of Zeus, Aphrodite, had not quickly
    noticed him,
his mother, who bore him to Anchises the oxherd.

---

30. It is perhaps significant, however, that while both Aphrodite's beneficiaries do escape destruction and survive the *Iliad,* their individual heroism, from an epic standpoint, has been permanently compromised.

She is expressly credited with protecting Aeneas from death, just as earlier she contrives Paris's escape from Menelaos at the fatal instant:

καί νύ κεν εἴρυσσέν τε καὶ ἄσπετον ἤρατο κῦδος,
εἰ μὴ ἄρ' ὀξὺ νόησε Διὸς θυγάτηρ 'Αφροδίτη,
ἥ οἱ ῥῆξεν ἱμάντα βοὸς ἶφι κταμένοιο·

(3.373–75)

And now [Menelaos] would have dragged him off
    and won an indelible triumph,
if the daughter of Zeus, Aphrodite, had not quickly
    noticed him.
She broke for him the oxhide chinstrap.

Thetis, like Kalypso and Aphrodite, is associated by the *Iliad* with impenetrable clouds and with veils and with concealment. But the *Iliad* does not pursue the parallelism of this aspect of their mythology. Thetis never spirits Achilles away from danger, and she never tempts him with immortality. On the contrary, it is she who states the human limits of his choice. Repeatedly, the absoluteness of the *Iliad*'s rejection of the idea of immortality emerges from its treatment, in relation to Achilles, of this protection motif, which figures so importantly in the immortal goddess-mortal lover or son stories and which has a preeminent place in Thetis's mythology.

Thetis acts on behalf of Achilles in the *Iliad* only after asserting repeatedly the knowledge that he must die and finally, in Book 18, the certainty that it is to happen soon. It is only then, after establishing her awareness of Achilles' vulnerability, her understanding that he cannot be saved, that she makes her gesture toward protecting him. She asks Hephaistos to create new armor for him, to replace the old armor worn by Patroklos and lost to Hektor. In contrast to the rescue efforts by which Aphrodite removes her man from danger, Thetis "protects" Achilles by providing him with the means to reenter the battle from which he will not return. The shield, supreme implement of "safety," becomes the instrument of his fatality. In its implications, this favor from Hephaistos corresponds to the initial one requested of Zeus: much as Zeus's acquiescence to Thetis commits Achilles to his death at Troy, so Hephaistos's repayment of what he owes Thetis equips her son for destruction and brings him closer to it.[31]

The *Iliad*'s treatment of the *hoplopoiia* is underscored by the evident existence of a similar scene in the *Aethiopis,* in which Memnon entered the battle wearing ἡφαιστότευκτον πανοπλίαν, prior to Eos's successful plea for his immortality. In the *Aethiopis,* apparently, Memnon's divine armor anticipated the successful intervention of divinity and was emblematic of its redemptive patronage. It confirmed Memnon's special relationship with the gods, which would make immortality possible for him.[32]

In the *Iliad,* the implement of protection made by Hephaistos at Thetis's request is the shield, which only

31. As we shall see below, Thetis is similarly owed a favor by Dionysos, whom she is said to have rescued as she did Hephaistos. Strikingly, his *antidōron* equally does nothing other than attest to Achilles' mortality: it is the golden urn in which Achilles' bones will lie with those of Patroklos.

32. See Griffin, "Epic Cycle and Uniqueness of Homer," 39–53, esp. 42–43 on immortality as a feature of the Cycle poems.

Achilles can endure to look at when Thetis brings it to
him. But it precisely does not fulfill for Achilles, as it
did for Memnon, the promise of ultimate divine preservation through the agency of his mother.[33] The *Iliad*'s
rejection of this outcome for Achilles, and hence for its
conception of heroism, is expressly stated. Thetis prefaces her request of Hephaistos with a summary of the
Iliad up to that juncture; the *Iliad* recapitulates itself here
from Thetis's viewpoint, so that it represents itself as a
mother's narrative about her son:

κούρην ἥν ἄρα οἱ γέρας ἔξελον υἷες Ἀχαιῶν,
τὴν ἂψ ἐκ χειρῶν ἕλετο κρείων Ἀγαμέμνων.
ἤτοι ὁ τῆς ἀχέων φρένας ἔφθιεν· αὐτὰρ Ἀχαιοὺς
Τρῶες ἐπὶ πρύμνῃσιν ἐείλεον, οὐδὲ θύραζε
εἴων ἐξιέναι· τὸν δὲ λίσσοντο γέροντες
Ἀργείων, καὶ πολλὰ περικλυτὰ δῶρ᾽ ὀνόμαζον.
ἔνθ᾽ αὐτὸς μὲν ἔπειτ᾽ ἠναίνετο λοιγὸν ἀμῦναι,
αὐτὰρ ὁ Πάτροκλον περὶ μὲν τὰ ἃ τεύχεα ἕσσε,
πέμπε δέ μιν πόλεμόνδε, πολὺν δ᾽ ἅμα λαὸν
ὄπασσε.
πᾶν δ᾽ ἦμαρ μάρναντο περὶ Σκαιῇσι πύλῃσι·

33. Much has been written on the importance of a hero's armor as an emblem of his warrior identity; see Ph. J. Kakridis,
"Achilleus Rüstung," *Hermes* 89 (1961): 288–97, esp. 292–93; on
the shield in particular, see W. Leaf, ed., *The Iliad,* vol. 1, 2d ed.
(London, 1902), 470. In *The Arms of Achilles and Homeric Compositional Technique* (Leiden, 1975), R. Shannon makes these connections: "Peleus' spear links Achilles with his mortal ancestry; his
new armor links him with his immortal parent and, through her,
with Hephaistos, its forger, and his attribute, fire" (31).

καί νύ κεν αὐτῆμαρ πόλιν ἔπραθον, εἰ μὴ
  Ἀπόλλων
πολλὰ κακὰ ῥέξαντα Μενοιτίου ἄλκιμον υἱὸν
ἔκταν’ ἐνὶ προμάχοισι καὶ Ἕκτορι κῦδος ἔδωκε.
                                    (18.444–56)

The girl whom the sons of the Achaeans picked out
    for him as a prize,
the ruler Agamemnon took back from his hands.
Grieving for her he was wearing away his heart; but
the Trojans hemmed in the Achaeans by the ships’
    sterns
and were not allowing them to go beyond; and the
    Achaean elders
beseeched him, and named many splendid gifts.
He himself then refused to ward off destruction,
but he dressed Patroklos in his armor
and sent him into battle, and supplied many people
    with him.
All day they fought around the Skaian gates,
and on that same day would have sacked the city, if
    Apollo had not
killed the powerful son of Menoitios when he had
    caused much harm,
in the front ranks, and given the victory to Hektor.

The Olympian reply, however compassionate, recon-
firms the inevitability of Achilles’ imminent death; divine collaboration on his behalf may honor him and en-
hance his stature, but it cannot save him and does not
propose to. Hephaistos replies:

θάρσει· μή τοι ταῦτα μετὰ φρεσὶ σῇσι μελόντων.
αἲ γάρ μιν θανάτοιο δυσηχέος ὧδε δυναίμην

νόσφιν ἀποκρύψαι, ὅτε μιν μόρος αἰνὸς ἱκάνοι,
ὥς οἱ τεύχεα καλὰ παρέσσεται, οἷά τις αὖτε
ἀνθρώπων πολέων θαυμάσσεται, ὅς κεν ἴδηται.
(18.463–67)

Take heart; do not let these things distress your
thoughts.
If only I were able to hide him away
from grievous death, when dire fate overtakes him,
as surely as there will be beautiful armor for him,
such as
anyone among many mortal men will marvel at,
whoever sees it.

Through Thetis the *Iliad* evokes this constellation of traditional elements—the divine armor, the protection motif—in order to violate conventional expectations of their potency, and it does so for the sake of the primacy of the theme of mortality, as Thetis's lament to the Nereids at 18.54–64 explicitly and deliberately reminds us:

ὤ μοι ἐγὼ δειλή, ὤ μοι δυσαριστοτόκεια,
ἥ τ᾽ ἐπεὶ ἂρ τέκον υἱὸν ἀμύμονά τε κρατερόν τε,
ἔξοχον ἡρώων· ὁ δ᾽ ἀνέδραμεν ἔρνεϊ ἶσος·
τὸν μὲν ἐγὼ θρέψασα, φυτὸν ὣς γουνῷ ἀλωῆς,
νηυσὶν ἐπιπροέηκα κορωνίσιν Ἴλιον εἴσω
Τρωσὶ μαχησόμενον· τὸν δ᾽ οὐχ ὑποδέξομαι αὖτις
οἴκαδε νοστήσαντα δόμον Πηλήιον εἴσω.
ὄφρα δέ μοι ζώει καὶ ὁρᾷ φάος ἠελίοιο
ἄχνυται, οὐδέ τί οἱ δύναμαι χραισμῆσαι ἰοῦσα.
ἀλλ᾽ εἶμ᾽, ὄφρα ἴδωμι φίλον τέκος, ἠδ᾽ ἐπακούσω
ὅττι μιν ἵκετο πένθος ἀπὸ πτολέμοιο μένοντα.

Alas for my sorrow, alas for my wretched-best-
childbearing,

since I bore a child faultless and powerful,
preeminent among heroes; and he grew like a young
 shoot,
I nourished him like a tree on an orchard's slope,
I sent him forth with the curved ships to Ilion
to fight the Trojans. But never again shall I welcome
 him
returning home to the house of Peleus.
Still, while he lives and looks on the sunlight
he grieves, and I, going to him, am all unable to
 help him.
But I shall go, so that I may see my dear child, and
 may hear
what grief has come to him as he waits out the
 battle.

The semidivine hero is inextricably associated with nonhuman perfection and scope, but instead of conceiving of him as elevated by this into the realm of divinity, the *Iliad*'s vision is of an exacting mortal aspect that exerts its leveling effect on the immortal affiliations and expectations of the hero. These retain their authenticity, but no longer their overriding authority as guarantors of immortal stature.

There is thus an additional dimension to the poem's evocation and adaptation of the aspects of Thetis's mythology and attendant motifs discussed above. The "violation of expectations," which is so effective on a formal level, provides the material of Achilles' own experience, as the poem represents it. In the *Iliad*'s characterization, Achilles lives the violation of expectations, of the assumption of what it means to be the goddess's son: to be

beyond compromise. Achilles' expectations, which this
assumption underlies—of the inevitable success of Thetis's intervention with Zeus, of the unambiguous privi-
lege of being τετιμῆσθαι Διὸς αἴσῃ (9.608), of the possibility of taking Troy with Patroklos alone—come to
be understood as illusions, and the course of the *Iliad*
describes their transformation. The poem uses Thetis
to underscore our recognition of this, as she replies to
Achilles' lament for Patroklos in Book 18 with an echo
of their initial exchange in Book 1:

> τέκνον, τί κλαίεις; τί δέ σε φρένας ἵκετο πένθος;
> ἐξαύδα, μὴ κεῦθε· τὰ μὲν δή τοι τετέλεσται
> ἐκ Διός, ὡς ἄρα δὴ πρίν γ᾽ εὔχεο χεῖρας ἀνασχών
> (18.73–75)

Child, why are you crying? What grief has come to
    your heart?
Speak it, do not conceal it. Indeed, these things have
    been accomplished for you
by Zeus, just as you prayed for earlier, lifting up
    your hands

To which Achilles responds:

> μῆτερ ἐμή, τὰ μὲν ἄρ μοι Ὀλύμπιος
>   ἐξετέλεσσεν·
> ἀλλὰ τί μοι τῶν ἦδος, ἐπεὶ φίλος ὤλεθ᾽ ἑταῖρος
> (18.79–80)

My mother, these things the Olympian brought to
    fulfillment;
but what good is there in them for me, since my
    dear companion is dead

The dislocation of which Achilles speaks here—and which constitutes his portion of suffering and of moral challenge—corresponds to the larger experience of the poem itself, in which individuals are compelled to revise drastically their formulations of their values and actions. Not only are the heroic code and the rationale of the war called into question, but central characters are repeatedly displayed in those moments of crisis that come to be recognized as typically Iliadic: the crisis of identity undermined by adamant revision of the expected and the familiar, a revision that assaults old roles and dissolves the continuity of the future. Helen on the walls of Troy or Hektor before them, Andromache preparing the bath, Patroklos storming the city: these figures are stamped with the poem's overriding theme. Achilles is preeminent among them, and his relation to this theme is both the most profound and the most fully documented of the poem. In its action the *Iliad* objectifies this preoccupation with inexorable events as a test of value, but the structure of the epic is studded with inner mirrors of this thematic concern. We read this larger question in every strategic violation of a "set" motif, as in the displaced outcome of the apparently traditional episode of the divine armoring.[34] The character of the particular altered expectation gives us its meaning, as the *Iliad*'s themes enforce it; the device of dislocation itself gives that meaning strength. Finally, the accumula-

34. See the analysis of J. I. Armstrong, "The Arming Motif in the *Iliad*," *AJP* 79 (1958): 337–54.

tion of characteristic incidents—sharing this revisionary quality of form and of theme—gradually establishes a distinctive tone that is yet another manifestation of the pervasive and unifying power of the determining themes. But the *Iliad* draws on tradition in order to assert as well as to alter convention, initiating its audience into an epic world at once familiar and unprecedented.

Thus the *Iliad*'s rejection of the possibility of Achilles' salvation through Thetis results in its emphasis on her helpless status, which is put into relief as a radical contrast to her part in the tradition of divine protectresses—one might even say, to her role as protectress *par excellence*; for the *Iliad*, in such provocative allusions as Achilles' speech at 1. 394–412, depicts Thetis as the efficacious protectress not of heroes but of gods.[35]

35. M. Lang, "Reverberation and Mythology in the *Iliad*," *Approaches to Homer*, ed. C. A. Rubino and C. W. Shelmerdine (Austin, 1983), 153–54, suggests that "hurlings out of heaven and rescues by Thetis seem to have been popular motifs," noting that Thetis "made a specialty of rescue (witness her deliverance of Zeus in 1.396ff., and her rescue of Dionysus in 6.130ff.)."

2

The Power of Thetis

The most startling silence in the voluble divine commu-
nity of the *Iliad* is the absence of any reproach made to
Thetis for her drastic intervention in the war. What accounts for Thetis's compelling influence over Zeus, and,
equally puzzling, for her freedom from recrimination or
retaliation by the other Olympians? From the standpoint of characterization, of course, for Zeus to accede
to Thetis's plea on behalf of Achilles means that the poet
can both show Achilles worthy of human and divine
timē and at the same time develop the figure of Hektor in
order to render him as an adversary worthy of the invincible Achilles; but it soon becomes apparent that no-
where else in the course of the poem is there an instance
of such far-reaching partisan activity on behalf of any of
the other characters. Such efforts as any of the gods may
make to assist either side inevitably meet with reprisals
and vituperation from one or more of the divine sup-
porters of the other party—as in the case, for example,
of Hera and Ares at 5.755ff.

Zeus continually reiterates his refusal to brook any
challenge to his promise to Thetis. All his threats against

the other Olympians that assert his supremacy on Olympos occur in this context.[1] Indeed, attempts are made on the part of Hera, Athena, and Poseidon to contravene Zeus's accord with Thetis by aiding the Greeks; and Athena voices her frustration at being unable to crush Hector:

> νῦν δ᾽ ἐμὲ μὲν στυγέει, Θέτιδος δ᾽ ἐξήνυσε
>   βουλάς,
> ἥ οἱ γούνατ᾽ ἔκυσσε καὶ ἔλλαβε χειρὶ γενείου,
> λισσομένη τιμῆσαι Ἀχιλλῆα πτολίπορθον.
>   (8.370–72)

But now [Zeus] is disgusted with me, and
    accomplishes the plans of Thetis,
who kissed his knees and took his chin in her hand,
begging him to give honor to Achilles the city-
    sacker.

Yet no complaint is made against Thetis herself; no mention is made of her less-than-Olympian status; no question is raised as to the appropriateness of her involvement in, as it were, the strategy of the war—in the way, for example, that Aphrodite's participation on behalf of Aeneas calls for caustic humor at her expense. How is the poem's audience to make sense of Thetis's extraordinary authority? It claims a divine consent—and consensus—that is significantly tacit.

In the previous chapter, I drew attention to the motifs

---

1. These raise repeatedly the specter of the Titanomachy, e.g., 8.477ff.

and attributes common to myths about immortal goddesses who have mortal lovers. As a rule, the goddess's
irresistible desire for her mortal partner is emphasized as
the vital impetus for their union;[2] thus Kalypso memo-
rably complains that the gods inevitably begrudge female divinities their mortal consorts, with perilous consequences for the latter. Thetis, by contrast, was not the
ardent seducer of her mortal lover. Her mythology gives
a wholly different cause for her uniting with Peleus,
which the gods in no way begrudged. In *Iliad* 18 Thetis
accounts for her uniquely grief-stricken condition:

> Ἥφαιστ᾽, ἦ ἄρα δή τις, ὅσαι θεαί εἰσ᾽ ἐν
>   Ὀλύμπῳ,
> τοσσάδ᾽ ἐνὶ φρεσὶν ᾗσιν ἀνέσχετο κήδεα λυγρά,
> ὅσσ᾽ ἐμοὶ ἐκ πασέων Κρονίδης Ζεὺς ἄλγε᾽
>   ἔδωκεν;
> ἐκ μέν μ᾽ ἀλλάων ἁλιάων ἀνδρὶ δάμασσεν,
> Αἰακίδῃ Πηλῆϊ, καὶ ἔτλην ἀνέρος εὐνὴν
> πολλὰ μάλ᾽ οὐκ ἐθέλουσα.

> (18.429–34)

Hephaistos, is there anyone, of all the goddesses on
   Olympos,
who has endured so many baneful sorrows in her
   heart,
as many as the griefs Zeus the son of Kronos has
   given me beyond all others?
Of all the daughters of the sea he forced on me a
   mortal man

---

2. So in the *Homeric Hymn to Aphrodite* (56–57), the goddess is
overwhelmed with passion for Anchises.

> Aiakos' son Peleus, and I endured the bed of a
>   mortal man
> utterly unwilling though I was.

Thetis did not choose Peleus, as Aphrodite chose Anchises; Peleus was chosen for her.

To what does the epic allude in these lines? What
myth is its audience intended to recognize? Can the
Iliad's reference here to the Olympians' endorsement—
even enforcement—of Thetis's marriage to Peleus clarify its representation of their reluctance to challenge her,
as she preempts the course of the entire war? To give
these lines their full weight—indeed, even to begin to
interpret them—means addressing other digressions that
interrupt the narrative surface of the poem.

In the *Iliad* Thetis has a present and, prospectively, a
future defined by the mortal condition of her son; as
such she is known in her dependent attitude of sorrow-
ing and caring. But the *Iliad* recognizes that she has a
past as well and in recalling it at crucial points suggests a
source for her role that is far more important than may
initially appear.

How does the *Iliad* reveal a character's past? Typically, it does so through the character's own reminis-
cences and reflections on his previous achievements or
position. But Thetis never refers to any past that does
not include her son. Instead, Hephaistos gives the only
first-person account of Thetis's previous activities, anterior to the time frame of the epic.

In Book 18, when Thetis arrives to request the new

set of armor for Achilles, Hephaistos responds to the
news of her presence with an account of how she saved
him after Hera cast him out of Olympos:

ἦ ῥά νύ μοι δεινή τε καὶ αἰδοίη θεὸς ἔνδον,
ἥ μ' ἐσάωσ', ὅτε μ' ἄλγος ἀφίκετο τῆλε πεσόντα
μητρὸς ἐμῆς ἰότητι κυνώπιδος, ἥ μ' ἐθέλησε
κρύψαι χωλὸν ἐόντα· τότ' ἂν πάθον ἄλγεα θυμῷ,
εἰ μή μ' Εὐρυνόμη τε Θέτις θ' ὑπεδέξατο κόλπῳ.
                                        (18.394–98)

Truly then, an awesome and honored goddess is in
    my house,
who saved me when pain overcame me after I had
    fallen far
through the will of my bitch-faced mother, who
    wished
to hide me for being lame. Then I would have
    suffered much pain in my heart,
if Eurynome and Thetis had not rescued me to their
    bosoms.[3]

3. That Eurynome, who otherwise does not figure in Homeric
epic, is named here as a participant in the rescue of Hephaistos
may be explained by the particular context of Hephaistos's con-
versation with Charis. Elsewhere in Homer, Hephaistos is the
husband of Aphrodite; but here Charis is his wife, as in the *Theogony* (945–46), where he is married to one of the Charites (there
specifically Aglaia; Homer uses simply the generic Charis). And
at *Theogony* 905ff., Hesiod identifies the Charites as the daughters
of Eurynome. The inclusion of Hesiodic Eurynome, therefore, is
owed to the presence of her Hesiodic child. Moreover, the mention of Eurynome here and perhaps even the presence of Charis
are motivated by what emerges, as I hope to show below, as the
theogonic context of references to Thetis's power. The *Homeric*

58   *The Power of Thetis*

In Book 6 (130–37), there is another instance of Thetis preserving a god from disaster; it is, similarly, not related by her but in this case by Diomedes, who cites it as part of an example of how dangerous it is to fight with the gods. Diomedes describes how Lykourgos chased Dionysos with a cattle prod until Dionysos in terror leapt into the sea where he was sheltered by Thetis:[4]

> οὐδὲ γὰρ οὐδὲ Δρύαντος υἱός, κρατερὸς
>   Λυκόοργος,
> δὴν ἦν, ὅς ῥα θεοῖσιν ἐπουρανίοισιν ἔριζεν·
> ὅς ποτε μαινομένοιο Διωνύσοιο τιθήνας
> σεῦε κατ' ἠγάθεον Νυσήϊον· αἱ δ' ἅμα πᾶσαι
> θύσθλα χαμαὶ κατέχευαν, ὑπ' ἀνδροφόνοιο
>   Λυκούργου
> θεινόμεναι βουπλῆγι· Διώνυσος δὲ φοβηθεὶς
> δύσεθ' ἁλὸς κατὰ κῦμα, Θέτις δ' ὑπεδέξατο
>   κόλπῳ
> δειδιότα·

                                (6.130–37)

No, for not even the son of Dryas, powerful
    Lykourgos,
lived long, who contended with the heavenly gods;
he who once drove the nurses of frenzied Dionysos

Hymn to Apollo (319ff.) gives a similar account of Thetis's rescue of Hephaistos, including her Nereid sisters but singling out Thetis as his benefactor.

4. For a discussion of the antiquity of this episode, and the poet's assumption of his audience's familiarity with it, see G. Aurelio Privitera, *Dionisio in Omero e nella poesia greca arcaica* (Rome, 1970), 57ff.

down the holy Nyseian mountain. And they all
scattered their wands to the ground, struck by man-
    slaughtering
Lykourgos, with a cattle prod; but Dionysos in panic
plunged under the sea's wave, and Thetis took him,
    terrified,
to her bosom.

Together with the episode described by Hephaistos in
Book 18, this account associates Thetis in a divine past—
uninvolved with human events—with a level of divine
invulnerability extraordinary by Olympian standards.
Where within the framework of the *Iliad* the ultimate recourse is to Zeus for protection,[5] here the poem seems
to point to an alternative structure of cosmic relations,
one that was neither overthrown by the Olympian order
(insofar as Thetis—unlike, say, the Titans—still functions) nor upheld by it (insofar as no challenge to the
Olympian order remains), but whose relation to it was
otherwise resolved.

We do not have far to look for explicit confirmation
of this in the poem. Once again, it does not come from
Thetis; she does not refer to her own power. Rather, it is
made part of Achilles' appeal to Zeus in Book 1, and it
stands out in high relief because of the anomalous form
of the plea. Why does Achilles convey his request to
Zeus through his mother, rather than directly? Such a

5. As at 21.505ff., where Artemis retreats to Zeus when at-
tacked and struck by Hera.

procedure is unknown elsewhere in the *Iliad;* and after all, Achilles is capable of appealing to Zeus directly, as he does at length at 16.233ff. But at 1.396ff. he addresses Thetis:

πολλάκι γάρ σεο πατρὸς ἐνὶ μεγάροισιν ἄκουσα
εὐχομένης, ὅτ' ἔφησθα κελαινεφέϊ Κρονίωνι
οἴη ἐν ἀθανάτοισιν ἀεικέα λοιγὸν ἀμῦναι,
ὁππότε μιν ξυνδῆσαι Ὀλύμπιοι ἤθελον ἄλλοι,
Ἥρη τ' ἠδὲ Ποσειδάων καὶ Παλλὰς Ἀθήνη·
ἀλλὰ σὺ τόν γ' ἐλθοῦσα, θεά, ὑπελύσαο δεσμῶν,
ὦχ' ἑκατόγχειρον καλέσασ' ἐς μακρὸν Ὄλυμπον,
ὃν Βριάρεων καλέουσι θεοί, ἄνδρες δέ τε πάντες
Αἰγαίων'—ὁ γὰρ αὖτε βίην οὗ πατρὸς ἀμείνων—
ὅς ῥα παρὰ Κρονίωνι καθέζετο κύδεϊ γαίων·
τὸν καὶ ὑπέδεισαν μάκαρες θεοὶ οὐδ' ἔτ' ἔδησαν.
                                                    (1.396–406)

For I have often heard you in my father's halls
avowing it, when you declared that from Kronos'
      son of the dark clouds
you alone among the immortals warded off
      unseemly destruction
at the time when the other Olympians wanted to
      bind him,
Hera and Poseidon and Pallas Athena;
but you went, goddess, and set him free from his
      bonds,
quickly summoning the hundred-handed one to
      high Olympos,
the one whom the gods call Briareos, but all men
      call
Aigaion—for he is greater in strength than his
      father—

who, rejoicing in his glory, sat beside the son of
  Kronos.
And the blessed gods feared him, and ceased
  binding Zeus.

A closer look at the context of this account helps to
explain why Achilles enlists his mother as intermediary
rather than addressing Zeus himself, as he does when he
makes his prayer in Book 16.[6]

6. Lines 399–406 of Book 1 have troubled critics since antiquity: Zenodotus athetised the passage, evidently sharing the
worry expressed in the scholia about the seemingly improb-
able alliance of rebellious gods, and preferring to read Φοῖβος
Ἀπόλλων for Παλλὰς Ἀθήνη. The attempt to overthrow Zeus
provided an opportunity for a variety of allegorical readings from
different vantage points, including the meteorological; see schol.
bT ad 399ff. and the discussion in F. Buffière, *Les mythes d'Homère
et la pensée grecque* (Paris, 1956), 173–79. Buffière writes, "Si bien
que l'allégorie a dû venir de bonne heure au secours de ce texte
scabreux, qui offensait doublement la divinité: car les dieux ré-
voltés péchaient à la fois contre les lois de l'ordre et la paix des
cieux, et contre les devoirs de l'entente familiale" (174). Thetis's
power, however, was never in doubt; she was allegorized as the
force ordering the universe: τὴν θέσιν καὶ φύσιν τοῦ παντός.
Some modern interpreters, less concerned about the particular
combinazione of deities or the impropriety of their behavior, but
more perplexed about the apparent absence of other references to
the episode of the attempted binding, have identified this passage
as an instance of Homeric "ad hoc invention"; see, for example,
M. Willcock, "Mythological Paradeigma in the *Iliad*," *CQ* 58,
n.s. 14 (1964): 141–54, and "Ad Hoc Invention in the *Iliad*,"
HSCP 81 (1977): 41–53. For an answer to "demonstrations" of
"invention" on the poet's part, illustrating "the extent to which
paradeigmata include inherited material" (Willcock, "Mythological Paradeigma," 147), see the convincing examination of this

We become aware that Achilles' appeal is remarkable
in a number of important ways when we note that the
passage is introduced at 1.352 with the following lines:

μῆτερ, ἐπεί μ᾽ ἔτεκές γε μινυνθάδιόν περ ἐόντα,
τιμήν πέρ μοι ὄφελλεν Ὀλύμπιος ἐγγυαλίξαι
Ζεὺς ὑψιβρεμέτης·

(1.352–56)

My mother, since you did bear me to be short-lived,
surely high-thundering Olympian Zeus ought to
     grant me honor.

It has been established that the typical structure of
prayers, as represented in archaic poetry, consists of an
arrangement of distinct elements: the invocation of the
god or goddess; the claim that the person praying is entitled to a favor on the basis of favors granted in the past
or on the basis of a previous response that implies the
existence of a contract between god and man based on
past exchange of favors; and the specific request for a
favor in return, including an implied or explicit statement of the relevance of the favor to the particular god's
sphere. This arrangement constitutes a formal communication of reciprocal obligations between god and man.[7]

---

passage in Lang, "Reverberation and Mythology," in *Approaches
to Homer,* ed. Rubino and Shelmerdine; also the discussion of inherited material about divine conflict in A. Heubeck, "Mythologische Vorstellungen des Alten Orients im archaischen Griechentum," *Gymnasium* 62 (1955): 508–25, on this passage, 519ff.

7. I am paraphrasing here from the detailed discussion of the
formal structure of Homeric prayers in Muellner, *Meaning of Ho-*

Achilles' prayer to his mother at 1.352ff. presents a variation on the formal restrictions governing prayers in Homeric poetry, as L. C. Muellner has shown. This is signaled by the substitution of δάκρυ χέων for εὐχό-μενος, the participle that regularly accompanies the prayer of a man to a god (although not necessarily requests from one god to another). Muellner observes that

> Achilles is depressed and helpless, his prayer is sub-standard, and his goddess mother makes an instantaneous epiphany. To express Achilles' sadness with particular force, the poet has replaced ὥς ἔφατ' εὐχό-μενος with #ὥς φάτο δάκρυ χέων. The deletion of εὐχόμενος may be a covert statement that Achilles is less a man addressing a goddess than a god addressing a goddess, or which is similar, a man addressing his mother who happens to be a goddess.[8]

Achilles' prayer to Thetis, as Muellner points out, omits the specific request for a favor. Curiously, we may note, it also lacks the element of a claim of entitlement to a favor implied by the "existence of a contract between god and man based on past exchange of favors."[9] *All* the requisite features, in fact, seem to be missing from Achilles' address to his mother; but they are pres-

---

meric EYXOMAI, 27–28. See as well H. Meyer, "Hymnische Stilelemente in der frühgriechischen Dichtung" (Diss., Cologne, 1933), esp. 9–16; E. Norden, *Agnostos Theos* (Leipzig, 1913), 143–76; M. Lang, "Reason and Purpose in Homeric Prayers," *CW* 68 (1975): 309–14.

8. Muellner, *Meaning of Homeric EYXOMAI,* 23.

9. Ibid., 28.

ent in the passage in which Achilles instructs her on how to approach Zeus.

The conventional form in which one god asks a favor of another does not include the reminder of a past favor or the promise of a future one on either part.[10] Conventionally, however, a god or goddess who makes a request of another god on behalf of a hero will recall the hero's past services to the god, as Apollo does for the sake of the dead Hektor at 24.33–34 or as Athena does on behalf of Odysseus at *Odyssey* 1.60–62.[11] But here, for Achilles' ritual or other services to Zeus, is substituted the reminder of Thetis's earlier championing of Zeus. Instead of asking for a favor based on Achilles' past, she is to ask on the basis of her own. It can be no trivial service that is recalled in exchange for reversing the course of the war, with drastic results that Zeus can anticipate; Thetis need say no more than

10. E.g., Hera to Aphrodite at 14.190ff.; Hera to Hephaistos at 21.328ff.

11. σχέτλιοί ἐστε, θεοί, δηλήμονες· οὔ νύ ποθ' ὑμῖν
   Ἕκτωρ μηρί' ἔκηε βοῶν αἰγῶν τε τελείων;
                                              (*Il.* 24.33–34)

You are relentless, you gods, and destructive: did Hektor never burn the thighs of oxen and choice goats for you?

   οὐ νύ τ' Ὀδυσσεὺς
   Ἀργείων παρὰ νηυσὶ χαρίζετο ἱερὰ ῥέζων
   Τροίῃ ἐν εὐρείῃ; τί νύ οἱ τόσον ὠδύσαο, Ζεῦ;
                                              (*Od.* 1.60–62)

Did Odysseus not please you, making sacrifices by the Achaeans' ships in wide Troy? Why are you so angry at him, Zeus?

Ζεῦ πάτερ, εἴ ποτε δή σε μετ᾽ ἀθανάτοισιν ὄνησα
ἢ ἔπει ἢ ἔργῳ, τόδε μοι κρήηνον ἐέλδωρ·
                                                    (1.503–4)

Father Zeus, if I ever before helped you among the
immortals, in word or action, grant me this favor.

Achilles, however, specifies wherein Thetis's claim to
favor lies:

πολλάκι γάρ σεο πατρὸς ἐνὶ μεγάροισιν ἄκουσα
εὐχομένης, ὅτ᾽ ἔφησθα κελαινεφέϊ Κρονίωνι
οἴη ἐν ἀθανάτοισιν ἀεικέα λοιγὸν ἀμῦναι
                                                    (1.396–98)

For I have often heard you in my father's halls
avowing it, when you declared that from Kronos'
        son of the dark clouds
you alone among the immortals warded off
        unseemly destruction.

Thetis, the rescuer of Hephaistos and Dionysos, was
first and foremost the rescuer of Zeus.

The most general, but most telling, statement of
Thetis's power is expressed by the formula λοιγὸν ἀμῦναι—"ward off destruction."[12] The ability to λοιγὸν
ἀμῦναι (or ἀμύνειν) within the *Iliad* is shared exclusively by Achilles, Apollo, and Zeus. Although others
are put in a position to do so and make the attempt, only
these three have the power to "ward off destruction," to
be efficacious in restoring order to the world of the

12. For a detailed discussion of the thematics of this formula,
see Nagy, *Best of the Achaeans,* 74–78.

poem. Thetis alone, however, is credited with having
had such power in the divine realm, for she alone was
able to ward off destruction from Zeus. She herself unbound Zeus, summoning the hundred-handed Briareos
as a kind of guarantor or reminder of her power:

> ἀλλὰ σὺ τόν γ᾽ ἐλθοῦσα, θεά, ὑπελύσαο δεσμῶν,
> ὦχ᾽ ἑκατόγχειρον καλέσασ᾽ ἐς μακρὸν Ὄλυμπον,
> ὃν Βριάρεων καλέουσι θεοί, ἄνδρες δέ τε πάντες
> Αἰγαίων᾽—ὁ γὰρ αὖτε βίην οὗ πατρὸς ἀμείνων—
> ὅς ῥα παρὰ Κρονίωνι καθέζετο κύδεϊ γαίων·
>
> (1.401–5)

but you went, goddess, and set him free from his
    bonds,
quickly summoning the hundred-handed one to
    high Olympos,
the one whom the gods call Briareos, but all men call
Aigaion—for he is greater in strength than his
    father—
Who, rejoicing in his glory, sat beside the son of
    Kronos.

That Thetis saves Zeus from being bound deserves
special attention; for the motif of binding on Olympos, together with the reference to Briareos, specifically
evokes the succession myth and the divine genealogy on
which it is founded.

The motif of binding is central to the account of the
succession myth in the *Theogony*, recurring as one of the
primary ways to assert divine sovereignty over a potential or actual challenger. Ouranos attempts to ensure his
power over Briareos and his other children by binding

them; ultimately they are freed by Zeus,[13] who in turn wants their allegiance in his own bid for hegemony. Their willingness to cooperate is based on their gratitude for being unbound:

"κέκλυτέ μευ Γαίης τε καὶ Οὐρανοῦ ἀγλαὰ
    τέκνα,
ὄφρ᾽ εἴπω τά με θυμὸς ἐνὶ στήθεσσι κελεύει.
ἤδη γὰρ μάλα δηρὸν ἐναντίοι ἀλλήλοισι
νίκης καὶ κάρτευς πέρι μαρνάμεθ᾽ ἤματα πάντα,
Τιτῆνές τε θεοὶ καὶ ὅσοι Κρόνου ἐκγενόμεσθα.
ὑμεῖς δὲ μεγάλην τε βίην καὶ χεῖρας ἀάπτους
φαίνετε Τιτήνεσσιν ἐναντίον ἐν δαῖ λυγρῇ,
μνησάμενοι φιλότητος ἐνηέος, ὅσσα παθόντες
ἐς φάος ἂψ ἀφίκεσθε δυσηλεγέος ὑπὸ δεσμοῦ
ἡμετέρας διὰ βουλὰς ὑπὸ ζόφου ἠερόεντος."
ὣς φάτο· τὸν δ᾽ αἶψ᾽ αὖτις ἀμείβετο Κόττος
    ἀμύμων·

. . . .

"σῇσι δ᾽ ἐπιφροσύνῃσιν ὑπὸ ζόφου ἠερόεντος
ἄψορρον ἐξαῦτις ἀμειλίκτων ὑπὸ δεσμῶν
ἠλύθομεν. . ."

(Hes. *Theog.* 644–54; 658–59)

"Listen to me, radiant children of Gaia and
    Ouranos,
so that I may say what the spirit in my breast bids.
For a very long time have the Titan gods and all
    those born of
Kronos struggled with each other every day for
    victory and power.
But show your great strength and irresistible hands

13. Hes. *Theog.* 501–2. References are to M. L. West, ed., *Hesiod: Theogony* (Oxford, 1966).

> against the Titans in painful battle, bearing in mind
> our kindly friendship, and all the sufferings you
>   returned from
> into the light, back from wretched bondage
> beneath the misty darkness, on account of our
>   counsels."
> Thus he spoke. And illustrious Kottos replied in
>   turn:
> ". . . Through your shrewdness, from beneath the
>   misty darkness
> we have come back again from our relentless
>   bonds."

With the aid of Briareos and his brothers, the Olympians, once they have managed to overpower Kronos and the other Titans, bind them and cast them beneath the earth.[14]

Binding is the ultimate penalty in the divine realm, where by definition there is no death. It serves not to deprive an opponent of existence, but to render him impotent.[15] Once bound, a god cannot escape his bondage by himself, no matter how great his strength. In this sense it is not finally an expression of physical strength (although violence certainly enters into the Titanomachy), but of what has been called "terrible sovereignty."[16]

14. Hes. *Theog.* 658ff.

15. References to binding of gods in the *Iliad* include the account of the binding of Ares by Otos and Ephialtes at 5.385–91, of Hera by Zeus at 15.19–20, and Zeus's threat to the other gods at 13.17ff.

16. On the metaphysical nature of binding, see M. Eliade, *Images and Symbols,* trans. P. Mairet (New York, 1969), chap. 3, "The 'God Who Binds' and the Symbolism of Knots," 92–124.

The attempt to bind Zeus recounted at 1.396ff. thus
constitutes a mutinous effort at supplanting him and im-
posing a new divine regime—on the pattern of his own
overthrow of Kronos and the Titans. Thetis's act in res-
cuing Zeus is therefore nothing less than supreme: an act
that restores the cosmic equilibrium. Once having loosed
the bonds, she summons Briareos, not to perform, but
simply to sit beside Zeus as a reminder of Zeus's final
mastery in the succession myth struggle. Briareos and
his brothers, in Hesiod (as later in Apollodorus), are
never instigators, but agents; Thetis's power to summon
the *hekatoncheir* ("hundred-handed one") here—beyond
what the insurgent gods are capable of—recalls Zeus's
own successful use of Briareos and his brothers. Not
even a single one of Briareos's hands needs to be laid
on the mutinous gods here: they are overwhelmed by
the assertion of sovereignty implied by the presence of
Briareos, rather than overpowered by him. In this sense,
one can see Briareos's narrative function as a mirror of
his dramatic function: he is a reminder. The binding element in itself is a sufficient allusion to the succession
myth, so that Briareos is included as a multiplication of
the motif.

Linked to this cosmic act on the part of Thetis is the
phrase ὁ γὰρ αὖτε βίην οὗ πατρὸς ἀμείνων ("for he is

On binding (and unbinding) as an expression and instrument of
sovereignty, see the discussion, with thorough exposition of the
comparative evidence, in G. Dumézil, *Ouranos-Varuna: Étude
de mythologie comparée indo-européenne* (Paris, 1934), and *Mitra-
Varuna,* 2d ed. (Paris, 1948), 71–85 (in English, trans. D. Coltman
[New York, 1988], 95–111).

greater in strength than his father")—a reference about
which it has rightly been said that "much remains obscure."[17] Yet some light may be shed on this "obscure"
phrase if we remind ourselves that the reference to the
son who is greater than his father is significant for
Thetis in a crucial dimension of her mythology.

The background of the fateful marriage alluded to in
Iliad 18 is given in fuller form in Pindar's *Isthmian* 8,
where Thetis's story is the ode's central myth.[18] *Isthmian* 8
recounts that Zeus and Poseidon were rivals for the
hand of Thetis, each wishing to be her husband, for love
possessed them. But the gods decided not to bring about
either marriage, once they had heard from Themis that
Thetis was destined to bear a son who would be greater
than his father.[19] Therefore, Themis counseled, let Thetis
marry a mortal instead and see her son die in war. This

17. G. S. Kirk, *The Iliad: A Commentary* (Cambridge, 1985),
95, ad 1.403–4. See pp. 93–95 for observations on 1.396–406. It
has proved difficult even to construe 403–4; in what way does the
phrase ὁ γὰρ αὖτε βίην οὗ πατρὸς ἀμείνων explain either of the
hekatoncheir's names? See the analysis by J. T. Hooker, "ΑΙΓΑΙΩΝ
in Achilles' Plea to Thetis," *JHS* 100 (1980): 188–89, who does
not consider the episode to be an invention of the poet, but rather
"a fragment of a poetical tradition represented elsewhere in the
Iliad" (188 n. 4, with references). On the other hand, perhaps the
phrase is not an etymological gloss, but rather explains the par-
ticipial phrase in 402—that is, it does not give a reason for why
Briareos is so named, but why Thetis summoned him.

18. Other references to the marriage are found in *Pythian* 3, as
well as in several odes written, like *Isthmian* 8, for Aeginetan vic-
tors: *Nem.* 3, *Nem.* 4, *Nem.* 5.

19. C. M. Bowra, *Pindar* (Oxford, 1964), 88–89, observes
that *Isthmian* 8 "is concerned with the consequences of what will
happen if Thetis marries either Zeus or Poseidon. If she does, says

divine prize should be given to Aiakos's son Peleus, the
most reverent of men. The sons of Kronos agreed with
Themis, and Zeus himself assented to the marriage of
Thetis.

ταῦτα καὶ μακάρων ἐμέμναντ᾽ ἀγοραί,
Ζεὺς ὅτ᾽ ἀμφὶ Θέτιος ἀγλαός τ᾽ ἔρισαν Ποσειδὰν
γάμῳ,
ἄλοχον εὐειδέα θέλων ἑκάτερος
ἑὰν ἔμμεν· ἔρως γὰρ ἔχεν.
ἀλλ᾽ οὔ σφιν ἄμβροτοι τέλεσαν εὐνὰν θεῶν
πραπίδες,

ἐπεὶ θεσφάτων ἐπάκουσαν· εἶπεν
εὔβουλος ἐν μέσοισι Θέμις,
οὕνεκεν πεπρωμένον ἦν φέρτερον πα-
τέρος ἄνακτα γόνον τεκεῖν
ποντίαν θεόν, ὃς κεραυνοῦ τε κρέσσον ἄλλο βέλος
διώξει χερὶ τριόδοντός τ᾽ ἀμαιμακέτου, Δί τε
μισγομέναν
ἢ Διὸς παρ᾽ ἀδελφεοῖσιν. "ἀλλὰ τὰ μὲν
παύσατε· βροτέων δὲ λεχέων τυχοῖσα
υἱὸν εἰσιδέτω θανόντ᾽ ἐν πολέμῳ,
χεῖρας Ἄρεΐ τ᾽ ἐναλίγκιον στεροπαῖσί τ᾽ ἀκμὰν
ποδῶν."
(*Isthm.* 8.29–38)

Themis, it is πεπρωμένον that her son will be stronger than
either. Here everything turns on the meaning of πεπρωμένον.
It is clear that it is not a decision of the gods on Olympus, but
something which is bound to happen unless they take avoiding
action. . . . What Pindar means is that, the gods being what
they are, such a union will inevitably bring forth a being stronger
than they. The gods have their own nature, and this is a consequence of it."

This the assembly of the Blessed Ones remembered,
When Zeus and glorious Poseidon
Strove to marry Thetis,
Each wishing that she
Should be his beautiful bride.
Love held them in his grip.
But the Gods' undying wisdom
Would not let the marriage be,

When they gave ear to the oracles. In their midst
Wise-counselling Themis said
That it was fated for the sea-goddess
To bear for son a prince
Stronger than his father,
Who shall wield in his hand a different weapon
More powerful than the thunderbolt
Or the monstrous trident,
If she wed Zeus or among the brothers of Zeus.
"Put an end to this. Let her have a mortal wedlock
And see dead in war her son
With hands like the hands of Ares
And feet like the lightning-flashes." [20]

Isthmian 8 thus reveals Thetis as a figure of cosmic
capacity, whose existence promises profound consequences for the gods. Not only does she generate strife
between Zeus and Poseidon because of their love for
her, but her potential for bearing a son greater than his
father threatens the entire divine order. The rivalry she
arouses between Zeus and Poseidon because of their

20. Translation from C. M. Bowra, trans., *The Odes of Pindar*
(Harmondsworth, England, 1969), 52–53.

love for her is unprecedented, but her greatest power does not lie there. Themis advises Zeus and Poseidon against marriage with Thetis, not in terms suggesting that their competition over her would be dangerous, but rather that marriage between Thetis and any of the Olympians (Διὸς παρ' ἀδελφεοῖσιν, "among the brothers of Zeus") would be disastrous in itself. If the issue were simply that of ending a conflict between the brothers, that presumably could be resolved by assigning Thetis to either of them. Once married to either of them, Thetis would be settled and beyond the other's reach; the possibility of her subsequently—δίς ("a second time")—causing a similar rivalry would be unlikely. But Themis fears another "banishment," the effects of a *petalismos*.[21]

Themis, the guardian of social order, is apparently trying not simply to avert a quarrel prompted by sexual jealousy between the brothers (a quarrel that would always be reparable), but a catastrophic *neikos* on the scale of previous intergenerational succession struggles.[22] This is what Thetis has the power to engender.

21. On the diction of banishment in the succession myth, see Hes. *Theog.* 491, 820. On the interpretation of *Isthmian* 8.92, see the scholion as given in A. B. Drachmann, ed., *Scholia vetera in Pindari carmina* (Leipzig, 1927), 275.

22. On the role of Themis, compare A. Köhnken, "Gods and Descendants of Aiakos in Pindar's Eighth Isthmian Ode," *BICS* 22 (1975): 33 n. 19. Apollodorus (3.13.5) says that one version attributes to Themis and another to Prometheus the revelation of the secret that Thetis will bear a son greater than his father: τὸν ἐκ ταύτης γεννηθέντα οὐρανοῦ δυναστεύσειν. We may recall the

Thetis's overwhelming potential as *Isthmian* 8 reveals it lies at the heart of Aeschylus's(?) *Prometheus Bound*. In the tragedy, Gaia (there identified with Themis) has made known to her son Prometheus the secret of Zeus's future overthrow: that Thetis, whom Zeus plans to "marry," is destined to bear a child who will be mightier than his father.[23] It is this threat at which Prometheus

---

rivalry between Hephaistos and Ares, as related in *Odyssey* 8, and the rapprochement of Hera and Aphrodite at *Iliad* 14.190ff. as examples of the reparability of quarrels arising from sexual jealousy. On the potential *neikos:*

Ζεὺς . . . ἀμφὶ Θέτιος ἀγλαός τ᾽ ἔρισαν Ποσειδὰν
γάμῳ.

. . . .
μηδὲ Νηρέος θυγάτηρ νεικέων πέ-
        ταλα δὶς ἐγγυαλιζέτω
ἄμμιν.

                                            (*Isthm.* 8.30, 47–49)

Zeus and shining Poseidon were rivals over the marriage
     of Thetis

. . . .
Let the daughter of Nereus not bring
     the petals of strife twice into
     our hands.

Note Themis's role in the *Cypria,* where *eris* also plays a crucial part. See Nagy, *Best of the Achaeans,* 253–75 and 309–16, on the overlapping semantics of *eris* and *neikos* and their implications for archaic Greek poetry.

23. R. Reitzenstein, "Die Hochzeit des Peleus und der Thetis," *Hermes* 35 (1900): 73–105, argues that Pindar and Aeschylus depend on the same early source, while Apollodorus makes use of a different, though essentially compatible, "Hauptquelle" for the story of Thetis; see esp. pp. 74–75 and 74 n. 1. See as well the discussions in U. von Wilamowitz-Moellendorf, *Aischylos Interpretationen* (Berlin, 1914), 132ff.; F. Stoessl, *Die Trilogie des Ai-*

hints, with increasing explicitness, throughout the tragedy, his private knowledge of which he asserts as the
guarantee of his ability to stalemate Zeus.[24] Although
we cannot be sure precisely how possession of this
knowledge may have served Prometheus in the trilogy
as a whole, we can say that the plot and dramatic tension
of (at least) *Prometheus Bound* are organized around the
Titan's knowing that Thetis is the answer to the only
question that matters to Zeus.[25] The secret of Thetis

schylos: Formgesetze und Wege der Rekonstruktion (Baden bei Wien,
1937), 146; and F. Solmsen, *Hesiod and Aeschylus* (Ithaca, N.Y.,
1949), 128ff., all of which argue for a common poetic source for
Aeschylus's and Pindar's treatment of the dangerous marriage
with Thetis. Solmsen (following Wilamowitz) points out that the
reference to Poseidon at *PV* 922ff. is gratuitous in terms of the
plot of the tragedy (Prometheus has nothing against Poseidon)
but serves to evoke the tradition about Thetis and the brothers'
courtship of her more fully. See also *RE* 19.1 (1937), 271–308, s.v.
"Peleus" (A. Lesky); Lesky comments, "Es unterliegt keinem
Bedenken, das Drama auf dieselbe Dichtung zurückzuführen wie
Pind. Isthm. 8 und die besondere Rolle des Prometheus aus der
Erfindung des Dichters zu erklären" (col. 296). D. J. Conacher,
Aeschylus' Prometheus Bound: *A Literary Commentary* (Toronto,
1980), 15, notes, "The myth of Zeus' pursuit, in competition with
his brother Poseidon, of the sea-nymph Thetis, was, of course,
traditional, but its connection with the Prometheus myth appears
to have been an Aeschylean adaptation."

24. Aesch. *PV* 167ff., 515ff., 755ff., 907ff.

25. Whether *Prometheus Bound* was part of a trilogy, and if
so, what the trilogic sequence and plots of the other plays were,
remains a matter for speculation. For a summary of views on
the problem, see Stoessl, *Die Trilogie des Aischylos,* 114–56, esp.
122–24. For a discussion and reconstruction of the trilogy from
the fragments (placing *P. Purphoros* first), see the appendix in
M. Griffith, ed., *Aeschylus: Prometheus Bound* (Cambridge, 1983),
281–305.

is represented in *Prometheus Bound* as indispensable to Zeus's survival: his rule, his future, are hostage to her fatal power.

While the danger to Zeus posed by the attempt of Hera, Athena, and Poseidon (1.396ff.), therefore, was averted by Thetis, she herself presented the greatest challenge of all to his supremacy, according to the myth as recovered in Pindar and Aeschylus.[26] The phrase ὁ

When and how did Prometheus divulge the secret of the dangerous marriage with Thetis? The scholion ad *PV* 167 indicates that Prometheus alerted Zeus as he was in full pursuit of Thetis in the Caucasus. According to Philodemus, *De pietate* (p. 41.4–15 Gomperz), Aeschylus made the revelation of Thetis's secret by Prometheus responsible for the latter's liberation (and for Thetis's marriage to a mortal); similarly, Hyginus (*Fab.* 64), who likewise explains that disclosure as the reason for Thetis's marriage to Peleus—although by this account the freeing of Prometheus followed only years (millennia?) later. Griffith, *Prometheus Bound,* 301, suggests that "the order of events (killing of eagle, revelation of secret, release of P.) is not certain but if [the scholion at 167 and a passage in Servius on Vergil *Ecl.* 6.42 about the killing of the eagle] are based on *Luomenos,* Thetis may have arrived, in flight from Zeus (like Io in *Desmotēs* . . .), thus provoking the still-bound Prometheus to divulge the secret before it is too late; whereupon Zeus gave orders for him to be released. . . . Or else Zeus' pursuit of Thetis may have been merely narrated (e.g. by Heracles or Ge)." The safety both of Prometheus and of Zeus, then, depends on Thetis.

26. It is necessary to proceed with the greatest caution when reading Pindar (or any later author) as evidence for traditions latent in Homeric poetry. Two considerations support the validity of doing so here. First, Pindar has been shown to preserve highly archaic material reaching back even to an Indo-European provenance, as illustrated in Benveniste's discussion of *Pythian* 3 in "La doctrine médicale," 5–12. Second, as C. Greengard, *The Structure*

γὰρ αὖτε βίην οὗ πατρὸς ἀμείνων at *Iliad* 1.404 describes Achilles within that tradition and recalls his association with the theme of ongoing genealogy and gener-
ational strife.

The *Iliad*, then, gives us a seemingly inconsistent picture. How are we to reconcile Thetis's cosmic capacity,
as alluded to in the *Iliad*'s digressions and as known to
Isthmian 8, *Prometheus Bound,* and Apollodorus (and the
traditions they follow), with what seems, for the most
part, to be her limited status in the *Iliad?* Our initial im-
pression of her there is that she is a divinity of at best
secondary importance, whose position is inferior to that
of the major deities in the poem. Her expressed grief
and reiterated helplessness in the face of her son's suffering make her seem vulnerable in a way that other goddesses are not. In comparison to Thetis's anguish, an episode like the wounding of Aphrodite in Book 5 (334ff.)
is a parodic one, which serves to illustrate that the
Olympians are beyond anything more than the most
transient pain. There is nothing anywhere in the *Iliad*'s
immortal realm comparable to the sorrowful isolation
of Thetis.

---

of Pindar's Epinician Odes (Amsterdam, 1980), 35, has demonstrated, *Isthmian* 8 "draws . . . heavily on the themes and move-
ments of the *Iliad* tragedy." Greengard's comprehensive analysis
concludes that "the diction itself of I.8 is more than usually allusive to that of the *Iliad*" (36 n. 27). It seems reasonable to suppose that Pindar in *Isthmian* 8 draws on mythology present in the
Iliad in some form, and recoverable from it—even if deeply embedded and only allusively evident to us. See the discussion in
Lesky's article on Peleus in *RE* 19.1 (1937), 271–308.

Her inferiority to the Olympian hierarchy is spelled out in Book 20. When Aeneas is reluctant to meet Achilles in battle, Apollo (in the guise of Lykaon) reassures him that he is entitled to challenge Achilles because his mother, Aphrodite, "outranks" Thetis:

> ἥρως, ἀλλ᾽ ἄγε καὶ σὺ θεοῖς αἰειγενέτῃσιν
> εὔχεο· καὶ δὲ σέ φασι Διὸς κούρης Ἀφροδίτης
> ἐκγεγάμεν, κεῖνοσ δὲ χερείονοσ ἐκ θεοῦ ἐστιν.
> (20.104–6)

Hero, come now and pray, you also, to the gods
    who live forever;
they say you were born from Aphrodite, the
    daughter of Zeus,
while he is the son of a lesser goddess.

It is this reminder with which Aeneas then responds to Achilles' taunts. He matches the account of Achilles' demonstrated superiority, Achilles' pursuit and near-capture of him, and his own flight, simply with the claim of his own genealogy, at 20.206–9.[27]

If we want to square the inferior place in the ranks to which the speeches of Apollo and Aeneas appear to relegate Thetis with the rest of her history as we have seen it, we may consider the suggestion in Erwin Rohde's *Psyche* (although Rohde does not address himself to this

---

27. For a thorough refutation of the view that this episode (and Aeneas's role in Book 20) must have been motivated by the patronage of a historical clan of Aeneidai, as well as an interpretation that reads it in particular relation to the confrontation between Achilles and Hektor in Book 22, that is, as integral to its context, see P. M. Smith, "Aeneidai as Patrons of *Iliad* XX and

particular problem) that an explanation for such disparity is to be found in the prevailing influence of pan-
Hellenism, through which the Homeric view of the
gods was shaped. The impetus of this unifying perspective, of which the Homeric poems themselves are a
monumental and influential example, is evident in the
Homeric poems'

> conception . . . and consistent execution of the pic-
> ture of a single and unified world of gods, confined to
> a select company of sharply characterized heavenly
> beings, grouped together in certain well-recognized
> ways and dwelling together in a single place of resi-
> dence above the earth. If we listened to Homer alone
> we should suppose that the innumerable local cults of
> Greece, with their gods closely bound to the soil,
> hardly existed. Homer ignores them almost entirely.
> His gods are pan-Hellenic, Olympian.[28]

While the deities whose cult-worship was most wide-
spread throughout the city-states are elevated to the superior status of Olympians, those divinities with a more
restricted range of influence are treated as lesser in importance and authority, however significant they may have
been in local belief. In this way local traditions remain
intact but are deemphasized, while the resulting gener-
alized pan-Hellenic conception is acceptable throughout
the city-states. The assembly of the gods before the the-

the Homeric *Hymn to Aphrodite*," *HSCP* 85 (1981): 17–58, esp.
(on this speech) 50.

28. Rohde, *Psyche,* vol. 1, trans. W. B. Hillis (New York,
1925), 25; see also especially 94.

omachy in which they all compete makes explicit the
subsidiary position of the locally powerful "gods of the
countryside." As Rohde points out,

> even the river-gods and Nymphs who are usually
> confined to their own homes are called to the *agora* of
> all the gods in Olympos, Y 4ff. These deities who re-
> main fixed in the locality of their worship are weaker
> than the Olympians just because they are not elevated
> to the ideal summit of Olympos. Kalypso resignedly
> admits this, ε 169f. . . . They have sunk to the second
> rank of deities.[29]

Thus the Homeric poems, subordinating realities of
religious practice to pan-Hellenic goals, systematically
demote such potent figures as the Nymphs—who, as a
group, in the *Theogony* occupy a lofty position appropriate to their tremendous stature and antiquity, being
the daughters of Gaia and consanguineous siblings of
the Erinyes and the Giants.[30] Hesiod also recognizes the
Nereids as occupying an elevated position in the divine
scheme, and we know of their importance in popular religion from a variety of other sources.[31]

29. Ibid., 50.
30. See M. L. West's discussion of the Nymphs in his edition
of the *Theogony,* pp. 154 n.7, 161 n.25, 199 n.130, 221 n.187.
31. E.g., Hdt. 7.191; Paus. 2.1.8 and 3.26.7. A related group
are the daughters of Tethys and Okeanos, who, however, number three thousand and are not all named. See West, *Theogony,*
260 n.337, on the *kourotrophos* function of the Nymphs. Hesiod
stresses their local nature by saying of their equally numerous
brothers, the rivers:

Prestige is denied them by Homeric epic, which either assigns these non-Olympian deities inconsequential roles in the narrative or demonstrates their subordinate status through a decisive confrontation with the Olympians. Such is the case of Kalypso in *Odyssey* 5. In the *Iliad,* a highly dramatic example is the battle between Hephaistos and Skamandros (Kalypso's brother in the *Theogony*), in which Skamandros is forced, improbably, to capitulate to the Olympian's superior might (21.342ff.). At the same time, the poem acknowledges the river god's intrinsic stature by calling him θεὸς μέγας (21.248), a title otherwise reserved for Olympian gods.

It may be the case that Thetis's stature in a local context is a factor in the *Iliad*'s reticence or indirectness of reference with respect to her power and prestige. Pausanias (3.14.4–6) tells us that she was worshiped with great reverence in cult in Laconia; this may be reflected in local poetic traditions, if Alcman's poem (frag. 5 Page) featuring her is a clue.[32]

τόσσοι δ' αὖθ' ἕτεροι ποταμοὶ καναχηδὰ ῥέοντες

. . . .

τῶν ὄνομ' ἀργαλέον πάντων βροτὸν ἀνέρ' ἐνισπεῖν
οἱ δὲ ἕκαστοι ἴσασιν, ὅσοι περιναιετάουσι
                                        (*Theog.* 367, 369–70)

So many other noisily flowing rivers are there . . .
It is difficult for a mortal man to say all their names
But the men who live near them know them.

32. Edited by E. Lobel in *POxy.* 24 (London, 1957), no. 2390, frag. 2; published as Alcman frag. 5 in D. L. Page, ed., *Poetae Melici Graecae* (Oxford, 1962); more recently as frag. 81 in C.

Thetis in the *Iliad,* however, is neither merely ineffec-
tual, like Kalypso, nor insignificant, like Leukothea; the
epic shows her to us as at once weak *and* powerful: subsidiary, helpless, but able to accomplish what the greatest of the heroes cannot and what the greatest of the

---

Calame, ed., *Alcman* (Rome, 1983). Known to us only through a
tantalizing commentary, Alcman's poem has been assumed by
modern scholars to be an early cosmogony and has been inter-
preted as such, following the reading of its ancient commentator,
according to whom the poem envisaged a sequence of creation in
which at first only undifferentiated matter existed; then Thetis,
the *genesis pantōn,* appeared and generated *Poros,* "the way," and
Tekmōr, "the sign." Darkness existed as a third feature, later followed by day, moon, and stars. With Thetis the creatrix as demi-
urge, this cosmogonic process involved not so much the bringing
into being of matter as the discrimination of objects, the ordering
of space, the illumination of darkness with light: an intellectual
rather than a physical creation. In the commentator's reading,
Alcman presented Thetis as the primal, divine creative force—the
generative principle of the universe. This aspect of Alcman's
poem has been discussed by M. Detienne and J.-P. Vernant, who
argue for a close connection between Thetis and Metis. See Detienne and Vernant's *Les ruses de l'intelligence: La Métis des grecs*
(Paris, 1974), 127–64, which develops a number of ideas first presented in Vernant's "Thétis et le poème cosmogonique d'Alcman," in *Hommages à Marie Delcourt,* Collection Latomus 114
(Brussels, 1970), 219–33. In various versions of their mythology,
Thetis and Metis have associations with bonds and binding; both
are sea powers; both shape-shifters; both loved by Zeus; both destined to bear a son greater than his father. Some scholars, like
M. L. West, have seen the name of Thetis as defining her role in
Alcman's poem; see West's "Three Presocratic Cosmologies,"
CQ 57 (1963): 154–57; "Alcman and Pythagoras," *CQ* 61 (1967):
1–7; and *Early Greek Philosophy and the Orient* (Oxford, 1971),
206–8. Detienne and Vernant, *Métis des grecs,* suggest that it is the
power of metamorphosis as an attribute that disposes these goddesses of the sea to a crucial cosmological role: they "contain" the

gods cannot.[33] The poem's explicitly and emphatically contradictory presentation of her leads to an explanation that addresses the interpretive process inherent in the *Iliad*'s treatment of the mythology it builds on, rendered more readily accessible to us through comparative evidence. The central element in the structure of Thetis's mythology, common to its representations in both *Isthmian* 8 and *Prometheus Bound,* is the covertness of her power; it is a secret weapon, a concealed promise, a hidden agenda requiring discovery, revelation. It is precisely this covert, latent aspect of Thetis's potential in cosmic relations to which the *Iliad* draws attention as well, both exploiting and reinforcing it *as allusion*.

The *Iliad*'s acknowledgment of Thetis's cosmic power,

---

potential shapes of everything created and creatable. More recently, G. Most, "Alcman's 'Cosmogonic' Fragment (Fr. 5 Page, 81 Calame)," *CQ* 37, no. 1 (1987): 1–19, has argued that although the extant commentary is cosmogonic, Alcman's poem was not. According to Most, Alcman's poem was a partheneion, whose mythic section contained—appropriately for its genre—an account of Thetis's metamorphoses when Peleus attempted to ravish her; it was her transformations that were allegorized by the ancient commentator as a cosmogony. If, as Most suggests, the partheneion context required some erotic narrative element—such as the "erotic rivalry" between the Tyndarids and the Hippocoontids in the fragmentary opening lines of the Louvre Partheneion—then it seems to me conceivable that Alcman may have used the framework of the Thetis-Peleus story as *Isthmian* 8 gives it to us: including not only the episode of the metamorphoses but the background rivalry of Zeus and Poseidon that necessitated assigning Thetis to a mortal mate.

33. In Book 24, Zeus must appeal to Thetis for the release of Hector's body by Achilles, admitting that the gods are powerless to rescue the corpse without her intervention.

known to these traditions, locates it in a past to which she herself does not refer.[34] Her grief is her preeminent attribute in the poem. Her references to herself, as mentioned above, are uniquely to her sorrow over her son. In contexts where we might expect reminders of her former potency—like that in Achilles' speech in Book 1— she claims for herself only suffering beyond that of all other Olympians. What lies tacitly behind the surpassing grief of Thetis, linking her past and her present in the *Iliad,* remains privileged knowledge, signaled by allusive references that are oblique, but sufficient. As we shall see in the following chapter, the *Iliad* makes her very grief a signifier of her former power, now suppressed or redefined. At the same time, by focusing on her sorrow as preeminent—while her power remains an allusion, displaced at the level of narrative—the poem locates its subject matter decisively in the human realm.

34. It is important to stress that we cannot assume a single common bearing on Thetis's mythology in Pindar, Alcman, Aeschylus, and Apollodorus (or, for example, Herodotus, who records at 6.1.191 that the Persians sacrificed to Thetis at Cape Sepias); but at the same time we may usefully draw attention to these authors' identification of Thetis as invested with vast cosmic power—an identification that clearly stems from elsewhere than the *Iliad*'s *overt* presentation of her. Thetis's silence on the subject of her own power is all the more striking in view of Achilles' description at 1.396–97 of her boasting about it.

3

The Wrath of Thetis

An inconsolable mother, unable to save her only child—
Thetis is the paradigm for the image of bereavement
conjured up with the fall of each young warrior for
whom the poem reports that the moment of his death
leaves his anguished parents forlorn. Shaped by allusion
to her mythology, however—its resonance augmented,
as we shall see, through various forms of reference—the
Iliad's rendering of Thetis makes hers a grief with a history; while in the poem's unfolding action Thetis's sorrow is conflated with that of Achilles: she laments not
only for her son, but with him:

> ὄφρα δέ μοι ζώει καὶ ὁρᾷ φάος ἠελίοιο
> ἄχνυται, οὐδέ τί οἱ δύναμαι χραισμῆσαι ἰοῦσα.
> ἀλλ᾽ εἶμ᾽, ὄφρα ἴδωμι φίλον τέκος, ἠδ᾽ ἐπακούσω
> ὅττι μιν ἵκετο πένθος ἀπὸ πτολέμοιο μένοντα.
>
> (18.61–64)

Still, while he lives and looks on the sunlight
he grieves, and I, going to him, am all unable to
    help him.
But I shall go, so that I may see my dear child, and
    may hear

what grief has come to him as he waits out the
battle.

Grief is never static, never passive, in the *Iliad*. Often
it is what motivates warriors to plunge into the thick of
harrowing battle, renewing their murderous efforts.[1]
For Achilles in particular, ἄχος (*achos*, "grief") is a con-
stant; and because it is linked to his wrath, his continuous
grief involves shifting consequences for other people.[2]
Achilles' capacity, as G. Nagy has shown, to effect a
transfert du mal through which his ἄχος is passed on to
the Achaeans and finally to the Trojans engages the
dynamic of his μῆνις (*mēnis*, "wrath"): "the ἄχος of
Achilles leads to the μῆνις of Achilles leads to the ἄχος
of the Achaeans."[3]

The *Iliad* marks the wrath of its hero with a special
denotation. Achilles is the only mortal of whom the
substantive μῆνις is used in Homer. In a study of the
semantics of μῆνις, C. Watkins has demonstrated that
"μῆνις is on a wholly different level from the other Homeric words for 'wrath.' The ominous, baneful character of μῆνις is plain. It is a dangerous notion, which one
must fear; a sacral, 'numinous' (θεῶν) notion, to be
sure, but one of which even the gods are concerned with
ridding themselves." Therefore "the association of divine wrath with a mortal by this very fact elevates that

1. See Fenik, *Typical Battle Scenes;* L. M. Slatkin, "Les amis
mortels," *L'écrit du temps* 19 (1988): 119–32, esp. 129–30.
2. See Nagy, *Best of the Achaeans,* 60–83, esp. 82.
3. Ibid., 80.

mortal outside the normal ambience of the human condition toward the sphere of the divine."[4]

Μῆνις thus not only designates Achilles' power—
divine in scope—to exact vengeance by transforming
events according to his will, but it specifically associates
Achilles with Apollo and Zeus, the two gods whose
μῆνις is, in the case of each, explicitly identified and
isolated as propelling and controlling the events of the
poem.[5] Significantly, in addition, Zeus, Apollo, and—
uniquely among mortals—Achilles are able both to generate and to remove ἄχος.

When Apollo and Achilles are involved in removing
ἄχος from the Achaeans, they are said to ward off λοιγός
(*loigos,* "destruction"). Apollo is appealed to by Chryses
to remove the λοιγός with which the god has afflicted
the Greek army (1.456). Achilles is requested to λοιγὸν
ἀμύνειν ("ward off destruction") where, as in the case
of Apollo, λοιγός denotes the plight into which he himself has cast the Achaeans: it is the term used at 16.32 and
21.134 to denote the Battle at the Ships. In fact, the successful capacity to λοιγὸν ἀμύνειν (or ἀμῦναι) *within
the framework* of the *Iliad* is restricted to the two figures
of μῆνις—Apollo and Achilles—who, like the third,
Zeus, can both ward off devastation for the Greeks and
bring it on them as well.

---

4. C. Watkins, "On ΜΗΝΙΣ," *Indo-European Studies* 3 (1977):
694–95 and 690, respectively.
5. Zeus's *mēnis* is referred to at 5.34, 13.624, and 15.122. On
the *mēnis* of Apollo, see 1.75, 5.444, 16.711.

The single other possessor of the ability to λοιγὸν ἀμῦναι successfully is Thetis. We have examined the passage in Book 1 that identifies her as the rescuer of the divine regime; she alone was able to λοιγὸν ἀμῦναι for Zeus, to protect him from destruction. But if the power to λοιγὸν ἀμῦναι is bivalent—if the one who wields it can not only avert destruction but also bring it on—then the threat posed by Thetis, who could λοιγὸν ἀμῦναι on a cosmic level, is potentially the greatest of all; for Thetis's ἄχος is supreme among the gods of the *Iliad:* the *transfert du mal* she might effect would be on an equal scale. Remembering that for Achilles ἄχος leads to μῆνις leads to the ἄχος of others, we may ask the question, why does the *Iliad* not predicate a μῆνις of Thetis? The answer, I think, is that it does—integrating into its own narrative by means of allusion and digression mythology that does not belong to the *kleos* of warriors.

If we consider the grief that Thetis endures because of the imminent loss of her son (whose prospective death she already mourns in her γόος [*goos*, "lament"] at 18.52–64), and her power to respond on a cosmic scale, we recognize elements that combine elsewhere in a context in which it is appropriate to show full-fledged divine μῆνις in action, namely in the *Homeric Hymn to Demeter*. The hymn is precisely about the consequences of the μῆνις that ensues from Demeter's grief over the loss of Kore.

Much as Thetis's grief is evoked instantly when she hears Achilles' lament for Patroklos in Book 18, prefiguring his own death,

σμερδαλέον δ' ὤμωξεν· ἄκουσε δὲ πότνια μήτηρ
ἡμένη ἐν βένθεσσιν ἁλὸς παρὰ πατρὶ γέροντι,
κώκυσέν τ' ἄρ' ἔπειτα·

(18.35–37)

He cried out piercingly, and his regal mother heard
  him
as she sat in the depths of the sea beside her aged
  father,
and she cried in lament in turn,

so ἄχος seizes Demeter at the moment that she hears her
daughter's cry as she is abducted into the underworld by
Hades:

ἤχησαν δ' ὀρέων κορυφαὶ καὶ βένθεα πόντου
φωνῇ ὑπ' ἀθανάτῃ, τῆς δ' ἔκλυε πότνια μήτηρ.
ὀξὺ δέ μιν κραδίην ἄχος ἔλλαβεν. . .

(*Hymn. Hom. Dem.* 38–40)

The crests of the mountains and the depths of the
  sea echoed
with her immortal voice, and her regal mother
  heard her.
Instantly grief seized her heart. . .

What follows is Demeter's wrath at the gods' complicity
in the irrevocable violation of Persephone, and through
that wrath both Olympians and mortals are bound to
suffer disastrously. Demeter isolates herself from the
gods, prepares full-scale devastation, and finally brings
the Olympians to their knees. Zeus is compelled to dis-
suade her, sending Iris with his appeal:

ἵκετο δὲ πτολίεθρον Ἐλευσῖνος θυοέσσης,
εὗρεν δ' ἐν νηῷ Δημήτερα κυανόπεπλον,

καί μιν φωνήσασ᾽ ἔπεα πτερόεντα προσηύδα
Δήμητερ καλέει σε πατὴρ Ζεὺς ἄφθιτα εἰδὼς
ἐλθέμεναι μετὰ φῦλα θεῶν αἰειγενετάων.
ἀλλ᾽ ἴθι, μηδ᾽ ἀτέλεστον ἐμὸν ἔπος ἐκ Διὸς ἔστω.
(*Hymn. Hom. Dem.* 319–23)

She arrived at the town of fragrant Eleusis
and found dark-robed Demeter in the temple
and addressed her, speaking winged words:
Demeter, Zeus the father, whose wisdom is
    unfailing, summons you
to come among the tribes of the immortal gods.
Come then, do not let my message from Zeus be
    unaccomplished.

But Demeter's *mēnis* is too great: she does not comply,
and Hermes must be sent to Hades so that Demeter may
see her daughter. Hermes reports:

῞Αιδη κυανοχαῖτα καταφθιμένοισιν ἀνάσσων
Ζεύς σε πατὴρ ἤνωγεν ἀγαυὴν Περσεφόνειαν
ἐξαγαγεῖν Ἐρέβευσφι μετὰ σφέας, ὄφρα ἑ μήτηρ
ὀφθαλμοῖσιν ἰδοῦσα χόλου καὶ μήνιος αἰνῆς
ἀθανάτοις παύσειεν·
(*Hymn. Hom. Dem.* 347–51)

Hades, dark-haired ruler of the perished,
Zeus the father bids you to bring illustrious
    Persephone
out of Erebos to be among the gods, so that her
    mother,
looking upon her, may cease from anger and dire
    wrath
against the immortals.

Among a number of striking correspondences between Demeter and Thetis, there is an especially telling
parallel in the κάλυμμα κυάνεον (*kalumma kuaneon,*
"black cloak") Demeter puts on as she rushes out in
search of Kore, which is subsequently reflected in her
epithet κυανόπεπλος (*kuanopeplos,* "dark-garbed").
κυανόπεπλος is used to describe Demeter four times in
the course of the hymn, within a space of only slightly
over one hundred lines, characterizing her at the height
of her ominous wrath, in the course of the gods' efforts
to appease her.[6] The final instance of the epithet occurs
after the joyful reunion of Demeter and Kore, but *before*
Zeus has appeased Demeter's wrath, promising her *timai*
and the return of her daughter for two-thirds of the
year. Once Demeter has agreed to renounce her wrath,
the epithet is not used again.

Demeter's dark aspect originates with the onset of
her ἄχος:

ἤχησαν δ᾽ ὀρέων κορυφαὶ καὶ βένθεα πόντου
φωνῇ ὑπ᾽ ἀθανάτῃ, τῆς δ᾽ ἔκλυε πότνια μήτηρ.

---

6. The epithet occurs at 319, 360, 373, and 442. κυανόπεπλος
is glossed by a fuller description of the goddess at 181–83, when
she has separated herself from the gods specifically out of wrath:

ἡ δ᾽ ἄρ᾽ ὄπισθε φίλον τετιημένη ἦτορ
στεῖχε κατὰ κρῆθεν κεκαλυμμένη, ἀμφὶ δὲ πέπλος
κυάνεος ῥαδινοῖσι θεᾶς ἐλελίζετο ποσσίν.

Disturbed in her dear heart, she walked behind,
with her head veiled, and her dark cloak
waved around the lithe feet of the goddess.

ὀξὺ δέ μιν κραδίην ἄχος ἔλλαβεν, ἀμφὶ δὲ
χαίταις
ἀμβροσίαις κρήδεμνα δαΐζετο χερσὶ φίλῃσι,
κυάνεον δὲ κάλυμμα κατ᾽ ἀμφοτέρων βάλετ᾽
ὤμων,
σεύατο δ᾽ ὥς τ᾽ οἰωνὸς ἐπὶ τραφερήν τε καὶ ὑγρὴν
μαιομένη·

(Hymn. Hom. Dem. 38–44)

The crests of the mountains and the depths of the
    sea echoed
with her immortal voice, and her regal mother
    heard her.
Instantly grief seized her heart, and she ripped
the covering on her fragrant hair with her own
    hands,
and around both shoulders she threw a black cloak,
and sped like a bird over land and sea,
searching.

This gesture of Demeter covering herself with a dark
shawl has been shown to signify her transformation
from a passive state of grief to an active state of anger.[7]

___

7. Full argumentation is given by D. Petegorsky in "Demeter
and the Black Robe of Grief" (unpublished paper), who clarifies
the distinction between the dying warrior being covered by a dark
cloud, expressed by such phrases as νεφέλη δέ μιν ἀμφεκάλυψε /
κυανέη (Il. 20.417–18) and μέλαν νέφος ἀμφεκάλυψεν (16.350),
and Demeter's assertive action in cloaking herself with her black
garment. Petegorsky compares Simonides (frag. 121 Diehl) on the
death of the heroes who perished at Thermopylae:

ἄσβεστον κλέος οἵδε φίλῃ περὶ πατρίδι θέντες
κυάνεον θανάτου ἀμφεβάλοντο νέφος·

In contrast to the image of the black cloud that sur-
rounds a dying warrior or a mourner, here the goddess's
deliberate assumption of the dark garment betokens her
dire spirit of retaliation, the realization of her immanent
wrath.

In this connection, the cult of Demeter Melaina at
Phigalia in Arcadia deserves attention. Pausanias reports
(8.42) that the Phigalians, by their own account, have
given Demeter the *epiklēsis Melaina* because of her black
clothing, which she put on for two reasons: first, out of
anger at Poseidon for his intercourse with her, and second, out of grief over the abduction of Persephone. Two
reasons—but her anger is the first. The Phigalians further explain that Zeus, having learned about Demeter's
appearance (σχήματος . . . ὡς εἶχε) and her *clothing*

οὐδὲ τεθνᾶσι θανόντες, ἐπεὶ σφ᾽ ἀρετὴ καθύπερθεν
κυδαίνουσ᾽ ἀνάγει δώματος ἐξ Ἀΐδεω.

To quote from Petegorsky's analysis, "what is crucial in the
poem is the change from a situation in which the cloud of death,
as a force beyond their control, consumes the warriors, to one in
which they have appropriated death by turning it into a willful
act—they are not passively slain, rather they choose actively to
die. The grammar reflects this change. The familiar dark covering
phrase is transformed from one in which the dark agent is the
subject of the verb of covering and the person who is to die is the
object, into one in which the heroes have become the subjects and
the cloud the object of the verb ἀμφιβάλλομαι. This is especially
interesting in that the verb which is used of Demeter putting on
the dark shawl is βάλλομαι, and it is said that she puts it on both
(ἀμφοτέρων) shoulders" (23). As the hymn proceeds to show,
Demeter is not passively overcome with grief; she is grief-stricken
indeed, but actively enraged as well.

(ἐσθῆτα ἐνεδέδυτο ποίαν), sent the Moirai to persuade
the goddess to put aside her anger (first) and to abate her
grief (second). Moreover, in their worship of Demeter
Melaina the Phigalians are said—by way of introduction
to their cult—to agree with the Thelpusian account of
Demeter's rape by Poseidon. This account, which the
Phigalia passage begins by referring to, Pausanias records
at 8.25.4–5 in order to explain why the goddess is worshiped by the Thelpusians as Demeter Erinus. After
Poseidon forced himself on her as she was searching for
her daughter, Demeter was enraged at what had happened and was therefore given the *epiklēsis Erinus* because of her wrath (τοῦ μηνίματος μὲν ἕνεκα Ἐρινύς
8.25.6). Demeter Melaina and Demeter Erinus are con-
gruent references to the same story: the black-garbed
goddess is a metonym of the wrathful, avenging goddess.

There is only one other dark κάλυμμα in Homeric
epic, and it belongs to Thetis. She wraps herself in it
when in Book 24 Iris announces Zeus's request that she
come to Olympos. Here the context is again, as in the
Hymn to Demeter, one of *achos.* Thetis replies to Iris:

> ἔχω δ᾽ ἄχε᾽ ἄκριτα θυμῷ.
> (24.91)

I have endless grief in my heart.

Because of her *achos* Thetis all but refuses to join the
other gods. Unlike Demeter in the hymn, she does respond to the summons; and yet the dark cloak she then
puts on expresses—as with Demeter—the active principle that her grief presupposes:

῝Ως ἄρα φωνήσασα κάλυμμ' ἕλε δῖα θεάων
κυάνεον, τοῦ δ' οὔ τι μελάντερον ἔπλετο ἔσθος.
βῆ δ' ἰέναι, πρόσθεν δὲ ποδήνεμος ὠκέα ῏Ιρις
ἡγεῖτ'.

(24.93–96)

So she spoke and, radiant among goddesses, she took
    up
her dark cloak, and there is no blacker garment than
    this.
She set out, and before her swift wind-stepping Iris
led the way.

The very request from Zeus acknowledges that Thetis
and Achilles together have, like Demeter, brought Olympos to submission. Thetis's potential for retaliation is
signaled explicitly: Zeus says, as she takes her place next
to him:

ἦλθες Οὔλυμπόνδε, θεὰ Θέτι, κηδομένη περ,
πένθος ἄλαστον ἔχουσα μετὰ φρεσίν· οἶδα καὶ
    αὐτός·

(24.104–5)

You have come to Olympos, divine Thetis,
    although sorrowing
with a grief beyond forgetting in your heart. And I
    myself know it.

῎Αλαστον (*alaston*), derived from λανθάνομαι (*lan-
thanomai*), means "unforgettable." The semantics of
ἀλάστωρ (*alastōr*) in tragedy, however, as well as the
morphological parallel with ἄφθιτον (*aphthiton*), indicate

that ἄλαστον can also mean "unforgetting."[8] In this
sense the πένθος of Thetis has the same ominous character as that of her son, whose final πένθος over the death
of Patroklos drives him to his devastating vengeance.

The image of the goddess taking up her κάλυμμα
κυάνεον may be seen, I suggest, as alluding to the implicit threat of μῆνις.[9] That Thetis wears a dark cloak
than which "there is no blacker garment," accords with
her having a cosmic potential for revenge—bivalent as
we have seen λοιγὸν ἀμῦναι to be—that is greater than
any other.

Why then does the *Iliad* not refer overtly to the wrath
of Thetis? Thetis, as observed earlier, never refers to her
own power, in contexts where we would expect it, but
to her grief. That grief, however, is twofold. When she
accounts for it most fully, to Hephaistos in Book 18, she
separates its two aspects:

> Ἥφαιστ', ἦ ἄρα δή τις, ὅσαι θεαί εἰσ' ἐν
> Ὀλύμπῳ,

8. Among other examples from tragedy, see Aesch. *Ag.* 1500–
1504. In *Comparative Studies of Greek and Indic Meter* (Cambridge,
Mass., 1974), 256–61, G. Nagy discusses the traditional comple-
mentarity of the themes of κλέος and πένθος and the morphology
of their epithets. See as well the analysis in Chantraine, *Dictionnaire étymologique,* 54; also the discussion of line 911 in volume 3 of
Wilamowitz's edition of Euripides' *Herakles* (1895; reprint, Bad
Homburg, 1959), 202.

9. Nagler, *Spontaneity and Tradition,* 27–63, has demonstrated
the symbolic signification of clothing and gestures related to it in
his discussion of Homeric *krēdemnon.* See also S. Lowenstam, *The
Death of Patroklos: A Study in Typology,* Beiträge zur klassischen
Philologie 133 (Königstein, 1981), on the symbolic force of gesture in the *Iliad.*

τοσσάδ' ἐνὶ φρεσὶν ᾗσιν ἀνέσχετο κήδεα λυγρά,
ὅσσ' ἐμοὶ ἐκ πασέων Κρονίδης Ζεὺς ἄλγε'
    ἔδωκεν;
ἐκ μέν μ' ἀλλάων ἁλιάων ἀνδρὶ δάμασσεν,
Αἰακίδῃ Πηλῆϊ, καὶ ἔτλην ἀνέρος εὐνὴν
πολλὰ μάλ' οὐκ ἐθέλουσα. ὁ μὲν δὴ γήραϊ λυγρῷ
κεῖται ἐνὶ μεγάροις ἀρημένος, ἄλλα δέ μοι νῦν·
υἱὸν ἐπεί μοι δῶκε γενέσθαι τε τραφέμεν τε,
ἔξοχον ἡρώων· ὁ δ' ἀνέδραμεν ἔρνεϊ ἶσος·
(18.429–37)

Hephaistos, is there anyone, of all the goddesses on
    Olympos,
who has endured so many baneful sorrows in her
    heart,
as many as the griefs Zeus the son of Kronos has
    given me beyond all others?
Of all the daughters of the sea he forced on me a
    mortal man
Aiakos' son Peleus, and I endured the bed of a
    mortal man,
utterly unwilling though I was. And that one lies in
    his halls, shattered by baneful old age. But now for
    me there are other sorrows:
since he gave me a son to bear and to raise,
preeminent among heroes, and he grew like a young
    shoot.

The primary cause of her suffering was being forced
by Zeus, the son of Kronos, to submit against her will
to marriage to a mortal. Thus the *Iliad* returns us to the
crucial feature of Thetis's mythology, her role in the
succession myth. She was forced to marry a mortal because her potential for bearing a son greater than his fa-

ther meant that marriage to Zeus or Poseidon would begin the entire world order over again.

Here once more there is a striking parallel with the
Hymn to Demeter, which stresses Demeter's anger not so
much against Hades as against Zeus, who ordained the
rape of Persephone by his brother. The poem is explicit
on this point. Helios identifies Zeus as exclusively *aitios*
("responsible") in the abduction of Persephone (75–79),
upon hearing which Demeter is said to feel a "more
terrible" ἄχος and to withdraw from the company of
the gods out of rage at Zeus:

> τὴν δ' ἄχος αἰνότερον καὶ κύντερον ἵκετο θυμόν.
> χωσαμένη δ' ἤπειτα κελαινεφέϊ Κρονίωνι
> νοσφισθεῖσα θεῶν ἀγορὴν καὶ μακρὸν Ὄλυμπον
> ὤχετ' ἐπ' ἀνθρώπων πόλιας καὶ πίονα ἔργα
> εἶδος ἀμαλδύνουσα πολὺν χρόνον·
>
>   (*Hymn. Hom. Dem.* 90–94)

And grief more terrible and savage entered her
    heart.
Thereupon in anger at the son of Kronos of the
    black clouds,
shunning the assembly of the gods and high
    Olympos
she went to the cities and fertile fields of men,
long disfiguring her appearance.

In the context of her wrathful isolation from the gods,
as noted above, elaborate mention is made of her black
garment.[10]

---

10. See *Hymn. Hom. Dem.* 181–83, quoted in note 6. It is perhaps worth adding that in Homer the formula τετιημένος ἦτορ
("disturbed at heart") when it is used to describe the gods always

The implicit wrath of Thetis has an analogous source. Given that the tripartite division of the universe is shared by the three brothers, Zeus and Poseidon on the one hand, Hades on the other, we see that these two myths share in the first place a preoccupation with the imposition and preservation of the existing hierarchy of divine power. Both the *Hymn to Demeter* and Pindar's *Isthmian* 8, in its treatment of Thetis's mythology, are equipped by the nature of their genres to emphasize this concern. Their other common element, namely grief over the confrontation with mortality, is what heroic epic uniquely elaborates.

The *Iliad* is about the condition of being human and about heroic endeavor as its most encompassing expression. The *Iliad* insists at every opportunity on the irreducible fact of human mortality, and in order to do so it reworks traditional motifs, such as the protection motif, as described in chapter 1. The values it asserts, its defini-

---

means "angry." When Hera and Athena sit apart from Zeus and refuse to speak to him for preventing them from assisting the Achaeans, they are said to be φίλον τετιημέναι ἦτορ (*Il.* 8.437); and when Hephaistos discovers the adultery of Aphrodite and Ares, he is described as follows:

βῆ δ᾽ ἴμεναι πρὸς δῶμα, φίλον τετιημένος ἦτορ·
ἔστη δ᾽ ἐν προθύροισι, χόλος δέ μιν ἄγριος ᾕρει.
(*Od.* 8.303–4)

He set out for his house, disturbed in his dear heart;
and he stood in the doorway, and savage anger seized him.

For a psychoanalytic perspective on the hymn's representation of Demeter's resistance to the patriarchal order, see M. Arthur, "Politics and Pomegranates: An Interpretation of the Homeric Hymn to Demeter," *Arethusa* 10.1 (Spring 1977): 7–47.

tion of heroism, emerge in the human, not the divine, sphere.

For this reason it is more useful to ask, not why the *Iliad* omits specific mention of a *mēnis* of Thetis, but why it gives us so much evidence for one; and why at crucial points in the narrative it reminds its audience, by allusion, of the theogonic mythology of Thetis as cosmic force. Questions of this kind may be said to motivate an inquiry like the present one, whose goal is to reinforce our awareness of how and for what purposes Homeric epic integrates diverse mythological material into its narrative, and how such material serves a coherent thematic imperative.

Thetis provides an intriguing example of the convergence of these dynamic processes, in that the way in which her mythology is resonant but subordinated corresponds to the Homeric insight that it literally underlies or forms the substratum of the heroism of Achilles. The intrinsic relation of parent to child, in which the parent's story becomes the child's story, is not banal here, but has special significance. The reality of Thetis's generative power has as its issue the fact of Achilles' mortality. In this sense *Isthmian* 8 describes where the *Iliad* should begin.

It has been argued by Watkins that whereas the *Iliad* demands the resolution of a wrath (whose religious stature is established by its very diction) in its initial thematic statement, the formula that would express such a resolution is rigorously suppressed. Suffice it here to quote his conclusion:

We have shown on the one hand the equivalence of
$\mu\hat{\eta}\nu\iota\varsigma$ and $\chi\acute{o}\lambda o\varsigma$ in the mouth of the one who says
"I," and the equivalence of $\mu\hat{\eta}\nu\iota\varsigma$ and $\mu\eta\nu\iota\theta\mu\acute{o}\varsigma$, for
which the latter is the tabu substitute precisely in
$\mu\eta\nu\iota\theta\mu\grave{o}\nu$ $\kappa\alpha\tau\alpha\pi\alpha\upsilon\sigma\acute{e}\mu\varepsilon\nu$ 16 62. We have shown on
the other hand that $\mu\hat{\eta}\nu\iota\varsigma$ in the sense of "anger,
wrath" is an echo, a phonetic icon of the forbidden
word $\mu\hat{\eta}\nu\iota\varsigma$. Everything then would indicate that the
dramatic resolution of the *Iliad* as a whole, whose
theme "wrath" is announced from its very first word,
is expressed by a formula "put an end to one's wrath,"
whose real verbal expression $\pi\alpha\acute{\upsilon}\varepsilon\iota\nu$ + $\mu\hat{\eta}\nu\iota\nu$ *never sur-
faces.* It is a formula whose workings take place al-
ways beyond our view, a formula hidden behind the
vocabulary tabu, a particular condition on the plane
of the parole, of the message, of the one who is speaking and the one who is addressed.[11]

Similarly, what informs the human stature of Achilles
is Thetis's cosmic, theogonic power—her role in the
succession myth; and although the *Iliad* never reverts to
it explicitly, it returns us to it repeatedly. If Themis had
not intervened, Thetis would have borne to Zeus or
Poseidon the son greater than his father, and the entire
chain of succession in heaven would have continued:
Achilles would have been not the greatest of the heroes,
but the ruler of the universe. The price of Zeus's hegemony is Achilles' death. This is the definitive instance of
the potency of myths in Homeric epic that exert their
influence on the subject matter of the poems yet do not

11. Watkins, "On MHNIΣ," pp. 703–4.

"surface" (using Watkins's term), because of the con-
straints of the genre. Nevertheless, the poem reveals
them, through evocative diction, oblique reference, even
conspicuous omission.

It is in this sense that we can understand what appears
to be a revision of the prayer formula by Achilles through
Thetis to Zeus in Book 1. The typical arrangement of
prayers as represented in archaic poetry, we remember,
consists of the invocation of the god or goddess, the
claim that the person praying is entitled to a favor on the
basis of favors granted in the past, and the specific request for a favor in return—based on the premise that
this constitutes a formal communication of reciprocal
obligations between god and hero.[12]

In directing his request for a favor from Zeus to
Thetis, Achilles has translated his reminder of a past
favor granted into *her* past aid to Zeus. But he prefaces
his request, and invokes his mother, by saying:

> μῆτερ, ἐπεί μ' ἔτεκές γε μινυνθάδιόν περ ἐόντα
> τιμήν πέρ μοι ὄφελλεν Ὀλύμπιος ἐγγυαλίξαι
> Ζεὺς ὑψιβρεμέτης.
>
> (1.352–54)

> Mother, since you did bear me to be short-lived,
> surely high-thundering Olympian Zeus ought to
> grant me honor.

In other words, Achilles' favor to Zeus consists in
his being *minunthadios,* whereby Zeus's sovereignty is
guaranteed.

---

12. See Muellner, *Meaning of Homeric EYXOMAI,* 27–28.

To reiterate, the *Iliad* reminds us of Thetis's mythology, through allusions to her power and through emphasis on the reciprocity of *achos* that she and Achilles share—his Iliadic and hers meta-Iliadic—in order to assert the meaning of human life in relation to the entire cosmic structure: in order to show that cosmic equilibrium is bought at the cost of human mortality. The alternative would mean perpetual evolution, perpetual violent succession, perpetual disorder.

The tradition of Thetis's power, the eventual issue of which is in the figure of Achilles, both enhances his stature and is subsumed in it. It thus represents the ultimate example of thematic integration. Heroic epic is concerned with the *erga andrōn* rather than the *erga theōn*. Thus with Achilles the mortal hero, the wrath of Thetis—potent in another framework—becomes absorbed in the actual wrath of her son. Achilles' invocation, in Book 1, of Thetis's cosmic power that once rescued Zeus must also invoke the power that once threatened to supplant Zeus; and once again, as in *Isthmian* 8, its corollary is the death of Achilles in battle.

That Thetis's power to persuade Zeus to favor Achilles has a source that the poem sees as located in an anterior (or extra-Iliadic) tradition is expressed not only in Achilles' speech in Book 1, but in a telling passage in Book 15. The result of Thetis's persuading Zeus to favor Achilles is the Trojans' success in bringing fire to the Achaean ships. In Book 15, at the final stage of the Trojans' advantage from the favor granted to Achilles before the death of Patroklos commits him to reenter the fighting, the situation is described as follows:

Τρῶες δὲ λείουσιν ἐοικότες ὠμοφάγοισι
νηυσὶν ἐπεσσεύοντο, Διὸς δὲ τέλειον ἐφετμάς,
ὅ σφισιν αἰὲν ἔγειρε μένος μέγα, θέλγε δὲ θυμὸν
Ἀργείων καὶ κῦδος ἀπαίνυτο, τοὺς δ' ὀρόθυνεν.
Ἕκτορι γάρ οἱ θυμὸς ἐβούλετο κῦδος ὀρέξαι
Πριαμίδῃ, ἵνα νηυσὶ κορωνίσι θεσπιδαὲς πῦρ
ἐμβάλοι ἀκάματον, Θέτιδος δ' ἐξαίσιον ἀρὴν
πᾶσαν ἐπικρήνειε.

                                                            (15.592–99)

But the Trojans like ravening lions
charged at the ships, and were fulfilling the bidding
        of Zeus
who continually roused great strength in them, and
        beguiled the spirit of the Argives
and denied them victory, but urged on the others.
For Zeus' intention was to give victory to Hektor,
Priam's son, so that he might hurl on the curved
        ships
blazing, unwearying fire, and accomplish entirely
the extraordinary prayer of Thetis.

Significantly, Thetis's prayer is qualified by the Iliadic
hapax ἐξαίσιον (*exaision*). It has been shown that the
phrases ὑπὲρ μοῖραν (*huper moiran*) and κατὰ μοῖραν
(*kata moiran*), and by extension the equivalent phrases
ὑπὲρ αἶσαν (*huper aisan*) and κατὰ αἶσαν (*kata aisan*),
are used in Homeric epic self-referentially, to signify ad-
herence to or contravention of the composition's own
traditions.[13] We may therefore observe that the exercise
of Thetis's power, with its massive consequences for in-

---

13. Nagy, *Best of the Achaeans*, 40: "Within the conventions of
epic composition, an incident that is untraditional would be ὑπὲρ

verting the course of the Trojan War, is ἐξαίσιον—
neither according to nor opposed to Iliadic tradition,
but *outside* it and requiring integration into it.

The *Hymn to Demeter* demands a sacral resolution in
terms appropriate to Demeter's wrath. Heroic epic demands a human one, and the *Iliad* presents it in Book
24. Thetis must accept the mortal condition of Achilles,
of which, as *Isthmian* 8 explains, she is the cause. This
acceptance means the defusing of μῆνις, leaving only
ἄχος. It is thus comprehensible thematically that Thetis
should be the agent of Achilles' returning the body of
Hektor, of his acceptance not only of his own mortality
but of the universality of the conditions of human existence as he expounds them to Priam in Book 24.

As such, Thetis is the instrument of Achilles' renun-
ciation of μῆνις in the poem. In a sense the submerged
formula παύειν + μῆνιν is enacted twice—not only on
the human and divine levels, but twice in time: in the
"long-time" eternality of the succession myth and in the
time span of the Iliadic plot. The intersection is the life
span of Achilles. With this perspective we can come to
apprehend the *Iliad*'s concern with the individual's experience of his mortal limitations and the existential choices
they demand, and equally its concern with their metaphysical consequences in relation to the entire cosmic
structure.

μοῖραν 'beyond destiny.' For example, it would violate tradition
to let Achilles kill Aeneas in *Iliad* XX, although the immediate
situation in the narrative seems to make it inevitable; accordingly,
Poseidon intervenes and saves Aeneas, telling him that his death
at this point would be 'beyond destiny' (ὑπὲρ μοῖραν: XX 336)."

4

Allusion and Interpretation

To the *Iliad*'s modern audiences, compelled by the urgent momentum of the poem's action and absorbed in the inexorability of its progress and the frontal intensity of its character portrayals, the epic's digressions from the imperative of its plot can seem to be a perplexing distraction, and its texture of oblique allusion and elliptical reference, of glancing, arcane hint and obscure, indirect suggestion can seem to be interlayered against the grain of its densely compact dramatic core. Where the *Iliad* has been described as subtly symmetrical in its formal construction, these features would appear to overbalance or recenter its inner patterning.[1] They have been accounted quirks of style: hallmarks of ancient epic, to be sure, but peripheral narrative features whose appearances have been justified as compositional "devices,"

---

1. On the structure of the *Iliad,* see, for example, J. T. Sheppard, *The Pattern of the* Iliad (London, 1922); and especially Whitman, *Homer and the Heroic Tradition,* chap. 11.

serving the exigencies of the bard's technique.[2] Thus an exemplary school text designed to introduce students of Greek to selections from the *Iliad* will, for instance, bracket Nestor's speeches and will propose that, if short of time, the reader may omit the Meleager episode; it will itself forgo including the entire story of Bellerophon.[3] The *Iliad,* in other words, may be satisfactorily introduced without such passages.

Our example of Thetis suggests that allusions, both abbreviated and extended in lengthy disgressions, are highly charged and repay scrutiny for the myths whose resonance or "reverberation" they carry into the narrative as a whole, signaling a constellation of themes that establish bearings for the poem as it unfolds and linking it continually to other traditions and paradigms and to a wider mythological terrain.[4] We might say that allusions provide the coordinates that locate the poem's action within a multidimensional mythological realm.

Evocations of the succession myth through allusions to Thetis's role in it ground the Iliadic theme of mortality in a complex set of divine-human relations. The *Iliad* presupposes an established hierarchy on Olympos,

2. See, for instance, G. Murray, *The Rise of the Greek Epic,* 4th ed. (Oxford, 1934; reprint, 1961), chap. 7, esp. 173ff.; C. M. Bowra, *Tradition and Design in the* Iliad (Oxford, 1930; reprint, 1963), chap. 4, esp. 84–86; also his *Homer* (New York, 1972), chap. 4; J. B. Hainsworth, *Homer* (Oxford, 1969), 31.

3. The otherwise extremely sound A. R. Benner, *Selections From Homer's* Iliad (New York, 1903) serves as an example.

4. "Reverberation" is M. Lang's effective term; see her article "Reverberation and Mythology," in *Approaches to Homer,* ed. Rubino and Shelmerdine.

but behind the static resolution that hierarchy represents lies a history of contention and struggle, as the gods themselves obliquely but forcefully remind each other. Zeus's authority is firmly in place. Claiming a preeminence that cannot be subverted, Zeus asserts that not all the other gods combined can dislodge him from his position of superiority. References to their past efforts to do so—or suggestions of possible attempts in the future—are reminiscent of such combats as are described in the Hesiodic version of divine competition for supremacy. Specific elements recognizable from the Hesiodic account are present in the *Iliad,* as in the passing mention of the monstrous Typhoeus at 2.782. But competition among the gods for power—and indeed reconciliation among them—is now, as it were, managed symbolically, through the partisan efforts of the gods on behalf of the mortal adversaries they favor. The gods' very participation in the war on behalf of competing human interests becomes an allusion to their own history: when they take sides against each other in the war, that is, in aid of Greeks or Trojans, their actions rehearse the older, larger conflict that digressions about divine strife have recalled.

There are, therefore, more layers of allusion than one, and in this sense the term "reverberation" is particularly expressive. Digressions about divine disorder echo another clash; they refer us to the ultimate contest for cosmic rule. Allusions form a system of evocation in which each reference produces not a single meaning but a sequence of overlapping significations—as with echoes, in which it is not the original sound but each subsequent iteration that is picked up and relayed. The direction of allusion may be reversed, proleptic: as when (for example) Hera refuses to renounce her intention to destroy the Trojans and their city, and Zeus resignedly accepts her intransigence but promises that in the future he will in return unhesitatingly sack whichever of her favorite cities he chooses—remembering her savagery toward his beloved Troy (4.30ff.). Here Zeus sets in motion a prospective allusion, anticipating an episode in the future that will allude to his present accommodation over Troy, and thus to their history of conflict.[5]

Such allusions as this, intertwining divine and human interests, bind past and future in a continuum whose effect is to blur the boundaries between digression and the narrative proper and to show the poem reasserting those boundaries by taking stock of, or reflecting on, its own plot. In the *Dios apatē* in Book 14, Hera's purpose is, literally, to create a digression, a countervailing movement against the narrative's momentum. Her seduction of Zeus is filled with innuendos of every kind, including suggestive hints about cosmogonic disharmony, as she enlists the services of Aphrodite and Sleep, and as she inveigles Zeus into thinking that the idea of their going to bed together is his.[6] Zeus appropriates the making of allusions, cataloging his former lovers (14.313ff.); and it

5. Similarly, Hektor at 7.81–91 anticipates subsequent retrospection over the death of the hero he expects to kill in the duel to which he challenges the Achaean chiefs.

6. See Janko's forthcoming *The* Iliad: *A Commentary,* vol. IV: Books 13–16, ad loc.

is these erotic references that are resonant, more than
Hera's staged reminiscence of Okeanos and Tethus, because they remind us of what we know from Thetis's
mythology: Zeus's omniscience fails in the face of his
own desire. Invincible and all-knowing, he is nevertheless baffled by eros. In the *Dios apatē* he is unable to see
beyond his desire for Hera: the digression *becomes* the
action; and the consequence is that the plot of the *Iliad* is
temporarily out of his control. Thus when he awakens
to find what has happened, his response has less to do
with punishing Hera than with reclaiming control over
the narrative: he declares what the plot of the rest of the
poem will be, and goes beyond:

"Εκτορα δ᾽ ὀτρύνῃσι μάχην ἐς Φοῖβος Ἀπόλλων,
αὖτις δ᾽ ἐμπνεύσῃσι μένος, λελάθῃ δ᾽ ὀδυνάων
αἵ νῦν μιν τείρουσι κατὰ φρένας, αὐτὰρ Ἀχαιοὺς
αὖτις ἀποστρέψῃσιν ἀνάλκιδα φύζαν ἐνόρσας,
φεύγοντες δ᾽ ἐν νηυσὶ πολυκλήϊσι πέσωσι
Πηλεΐδεω Ἀχιλῆος· ὁ δ᾽ ἀναστήσει ὃν ἑταῖρον
Πάτροκλον· τὸν δὲ κτενεῖ ἔγχεϊ φαίδιμος "Εκτωρ
Ἰλίου προπάροιθε, πολέας ὀλέσαντ᾽ αἰζηοὺς
τοὺς ἄλλους, μετὰ δ᾽ υἱὸν ἐμὸν Σαρπηδόνα δῖον.
τοῦ δὲ χολωσάμενος κτενεῖ "Εκτορα δῖος
            Ἀχιλλεύς.
ἐκ τοῦ δ᾽ ἄν τοι ἔπειτα παλίωξιν παρὰ νηῶν
αἰὲν ἐγὼ τεύχοιμι διαμπερές, εἰς ὅ κ᾽ Ἀχαιοὶ
"Ιλιον αἰπὺ ἕλοιεν Ἀθηναίης διὰ βουλάς.
                                    (15.59–71)

Let Phoibos Apollo rouse Hektor into battle
and again breathe strength into him, and make him
    forget the pains

that now wear down his spirit; let him meanwhile
      turn the Achaeans
back again, urging them to unresisting panic,
and let them, fleeing, fall among the benched ships
of Achilles, son of Peleus. And he shall send out his
      companion
Patroklos; but him shining Hektor shall kill with the
      spear
before Ilion, once Patroklos has killed many other
      young men, among them my son, radiant
      Sarpedon.
And angered because of Patroklos, brilliant Achilles
      shall kill Hektor.
From that point I shall contrive a continuous, steady
retreat from the ships, until the Achaeans
capture steep Ilion through the plans of Athena.

But if the divine battlefield has become the human battlefield, it is not that the *Iliad* represents the suffering of
its characters merely as a function—or as a reenactment
at one remove—of divine dissatisfactions. Allusions to
Thetis's mythology in particular, continually retroject-
ing into a pre-Iliadic past the process of resolving divine
discord, help to evoke stages in an evolution of cosmic
order in which men have had a part—in which there is a
place for the human condition. In the Hesiodic version
of the achievement of hegemony on Olympos in the
Theogony, Zeus averts the predicted challenge of a child
who will overmaster him by swallowing one goddess
and giving birth to another; men are not in the picture.[7]

7. The mysterious threat of a son, at *Theogony* 897–98, never
materializes.

The solution implicit in the mythology of Thetis, by contrast, posits a relationship between the achieved stability of the divine order and the mutability of the human order, where each generation must yield to the next. Allusions recalling hostility and competition among the gods, then—far from serving either to burlesque the drama at Troy or to emphasize the gods' role as vicarious spectators—link divine and human in a profoundly reciprocal connection, pointing to an intersection between the two that accounts for the gods' stake in the war as other than that of detached, if sentimental, onlookers.

Viewed from the vantage point of the mythology they recover, the digressions that encase these evocative allusions—in some instances at length—take on a different aspect from that assigned them in many recent studies of the subject, among them Erich Auerbach's memorable opening essay in *Mimesis*.[8] Citing correspondence between Goethe and Schiller on the digressive mode of epic, Auerbach affirms his own sense that Homeric style is not impelled by "any tensional and suspensive striving toward a goal." Yet he proposes that the origins of the digressive style must be accounted for not so much in terms of its peculiar effect on the movement of the plot, but more as a consequence of a characteristic Homeric phenomenology: an object (or character, or action) is constituted by whatever can be expressed about it on the surface. Auerbach explains: "The basic impulse of the Homeric style . . . [is] to represent phenomena in fully externalized form, visible and palpable in all their

8. E. Auerbach, *Mimesis* (Princeton, 1953), chap. 1, 1–20.

parts." Observing that the long passage in *Odyssey* 19 that describes how Odysseus acquired his distinguishing scar might easily have been recounted not as part of the "externalizing" descriptive narrative but as a recollection voiced by Odysseus himself, Auerbach elaborates: "But any such subjectivist-perspectivist procedure, creating a foreground and background, resulting in the present lying open to the depths of the past, is entirely foreign to the Homeric style; Homeric style knows only a foreground, only a uniformly illuminated, uniformly objective present."[9]

As our understanding of the distinctive properties of oral traditional poetry has grown over the past several decades, however, we have come increasingly to see that—as the present study aims to demonstrate—fundamental to the poetics of compositions like the *Iliad* and *Odyssey* is a process of selection, combination, and adaptation that draws out the full resonance and evocative power of the mythological material the poems incorporate. To an audience familiar with the mythological corpus available to the poet, the digressions create a topography the recesses of which reveal a rich and dense foundation beneath the evenly illuminated surface Auerbach describes. The more we are able to perceive the range and coherence of the references themselves, the more we can see how they serve to provide a context and a perspective in which to account for—to make sense of—character, action, and theme.

9. Ibid., 3, 4, and 5, respectively.

For all that he may underestimate the background they constitute and the shadows cast by the very obliqueness of their allusive representation, Auerbach himself clearly perceives that the continuous integration of mythological passages supplementing (although they appear to delay) the poem's narrative progress must be appreciated as the reflection, on the level of style, of a distinctive way of seeing and comprehending epic personages and events in their totality. This mode, which Auerbach takes to be characteristically Homeric, we may recognize, in all its cognitive dimensions, as intrinsic to traditional literature of the archaic period, including the poetry of Hesiod, the Homeric hymns, and Pindar.

More recent discussion has concentrated on the relationship of digressions to the exigencies of their immediate narrative situation.[10] Students of the subject have

10. So, for example, Willcock, "Mythological Paradeigma," followed by B. K. Braswell, "Mythological Innovation in the *Iliad*," *CQ* 21 (1971): 16–26. In a subsequent article, "Ad Hoc Invention," 43, Willcock describes his earlier study as "endeavor-[ing] to show that Homer has a genial habit of inventing mythology for the purpose of adducing it as a parallel to the situation in his story." In this article, which supports the original thesis by explaining "invention" as an inevitable consequence of "formulaic composition," Willcock concludes that "the oral poet concentrates on the particular scene which he is describing. He does his best to make it acceptable, producing corroborative evidence and circumstantial details as he requires them to that end" (45). N. Austin's perceptive study "The Function of Digressions in the *Iliad*," *GRBS* 7, no. 4 (1966): 295–312, emphasizes the role of digressions in "concentrat[ing] tension" at "high points in the drama," so as to create "dramatic urgency" (311–12). A. Köhnken, in his thoughtful discussion of Auerbach's essay in "Die Narbe

focused in particular on the function of digressions as
paradeigmata exploited in a rhetorical strategy designed
to persuade an addressee toward or away from a particular action. Attention has been fixed so determinedly on
this point that it has led some scholars to the conclusion
that the mythological allusions employed in hortatory
situations were "ad hoc" inventions, improvised by the
poet to offer his characters greater rhetorical power.[11] It
is certainly true that our sources for identifying and
piecing together the mythology underlying any number
of epic allusions are limited and that the subtlety and
virtuosity with which fragmentary references are worked
into the poem may make it difficult to know even where
to look for the appropriate sources, especially because
the more familiar a reference was to the Homeric audience, the more abbreviated or schematic its presentation
is likely to be. Yet to infer that allusions for which we
have no other corroborating text are inventions devised
for the sake of the immediate context is only one—and
perhaps not the most far-reaching—approach to the
workings of traditional narrative. Indeed, the logic of an
argument that puts emphasis on the hortatory context
for mythological allusions would seem to require that in
such contexts the most familiar, recognizable exemplars
would be cited as instruments of persuasion; presum-

des Odysseus: Ein Beitrag zur homerisch-epischen Erzähltechnik," *AuA* 22.2 (1976): 101–14, also assigns priority to the narrative circumstances as giving significance to the digressions; see
esp. pp. 107–8.
    11. See especially Willcock, "Ad Hoc Invention."

ably a speaker would most effectively advert to a paradigm that had obvious meaning for his audience, in order to compel assent.[12]

As analyses of such digressions as the Meleager episode have shown, details may be suppressed, highlighted, or significantly rearranged; and as we see from the multiple versions of the Oresteia story within the *Odyssey,* the speaker's point of view may be shown by the poet to be a factor in the shading of details of a well-known model.[13] Beyond their utility for the speaker, however, is their meaning for the narrative as a whole; much as the Oresteia story has meaning that includes, but does not end with, what any individual speaker intends, its themes of seduction, betrayal, and the disintegration of the *oikos* are resonant beyond the persuasive or dissuasive goals of a particular narrator. Rather than assuming, then, that mythological precedents are invented "ad hoc" to suit the speaker's particular hortatory injunction, it would be equally possible to suppose that the rhetorical situation is created as a vehicle to introduce and frame mythological material valuable for its thematic impact.

The *Iliad*'s fundamental narrative mode of evocation

12. Thus the address of Nestor to Agamemnon and Achilles at 1.254ff. would have seemed an effective place to interpolate a reference to Theseus. On 1.265 as a later, Athenian addition, see Kirk, *The Iliad: A Commentary* ad. loc.

13. See the discussion in Kakridis, *Homeric Researches,* chap. 1; N. Felson-Rubin, "Penelope's Perspectives: Character from Plot," in *Beyond Oral Poetry,* ed. J. M. Bremer, I. J. F. de Jong, J. Kalff (Amsterdam, 1987), 61–83.

elicits from its audience a particular kind of recognition that retrieves as full a context as possible for each fragmentary reference: a process of continuous recollection operating simultaneously with the audience's anticipation and apprehension of the developments of the poem's plot. As this study has aimed to illustrate, allusions remind the audience of other enriching traditions and serve to alert us to instances not of invention but of selection and adaptation. The *Dios boulē,* with which the poem opens, itself alludes, it has been convincingly argued, to a tradition explicit outside the *Iliad* with which its audience would have been well acquainted.[14] Proclus's summary of the *Cypria,* at the beginning of the Epic Cycle, mentions Zeus's taking counsel to arrange the Trojan War.[15] More specifically, a scholion at 1.5 gives a *historia* ascribing to the *Cypria* the account of a grand plan devised by Zeus to lessen the oppression suffered by Earth because of overpopulation and to punish men for their lack of piety. War is to be the remedy, war generated by Thetis's marriage to a mortal.[16] The scho-

14. See W. Kullmann, "Ein vorhomerisches Motiv im Iliasproömium," *Philologus* 99 (1955): 167–92, as well as "Zur ΔΙΟΣ ΒΟΥΛΗ des Iliasproömiums," *Philologus* 100 (1956): 132–33.

15. With Themis or Thetis? See A. Severyns, "Sur le début des chants cypriens," *Mededelingen der Koninklijke Nederlandse Akademie van Wetenschappen, afd. Letterkunde* n.s. 28, no. 5 (1965): 285–89.

16. See schol. AD ad A 5–6. Thetis's marriage is called *Thetidos thnētogamian;* for the text, see A. Ludwich, *Textkritische Untersuchungen über die mythologischen Scholien zu Homers* Ilias, vol. 1 (Königsberg, 1900), 10–11.

lion proceeds to quote seven lines from the *Cypria* as il-
lustration, in which Zeus's solution for relieving Earth's
burden is specified: it is the Trojan War; the heroes will
perish at Troy.

The encompassing implications of this reference may
be echoed in two proleptic digressions later in the poem.
It has been shown that the passages in Books 7 and 12
about the obliteration of the Achaean wall by Poseidon
and Apollo evoke nothing less than the conjoined themes
of mankind's destruction and of heroic glory, by alluding to a mythological complex linking the plan of Zeus,
the separation of men from gods, the demise of the
demigods, the end of the Golden Age, and the threat of
a universal deluge.[17]

With the image of divinely orchestrated devastation
prefigured in the passage at 12.3–33, "the poem places
its events far away in a past which becomes remote and
fated not only to end, but to vanish."[18] The passage
concludes as follows:

όφρα μὲν Ἕκτωρ ζωὸς ἔην καὶ μήνι' Ἀχιλλεὺς
καὶ Πριάμοιο ἄνακτος ἀπόρθητος πόλις ἔπλεν,
τόφρα δὲ καὶ μέγα τεῖχος Ἀχαιῶν ἔμπεδον ἦεν.
αὐτὰρ ἐπεὶ κατὰ μὲν Τρώων θάνον ὅσσοι ἄριστοι,
πολλοὶ δ' Ἀργείων οἱ μὲν δάμεν, οἱ δὲ λίποντο,
πέρθετο δὲ Πριάμοιο πόλις δεκάτῳ ἐνιαυτῷ,
Ἀργεῖοι δ' ἐν νηυσὶ φίλην ἐς πατρίδ' ἔβησαν,
δὴ τότε μητιόωντο Ποσειδάων καὶ Ἀπόλλων

17. I refer to Scodel's important article "The Achaean Wall and
the Myth of Destruction."
18. Scodel, "Achaean Wall and Myth of Destruction," 48.

τεῖχος ἀμαλδῦναι, ποταμῶν μένος εἰσαγαγόντες.
ὅσσοι ἀπ᾽ Ἰδαίων ὀρέων ἅλαδε προρέουσι,
Ῥῆσός θ᾽ Ἑπτάπορός τε Κάρησός τε Ῥοδίος τε
Γρήνικός τε καὶ Αἴσηπος δῖός τε Σκάμανδρος
καὶ Σιμόεις, ὅθι πολλὰ βοάγρια καὶ τρυφάλειαι
κάππεσον ἐν κονίῃσι καὶ ἡμιθέων γένος ἀνδρῶν·
τῶν πάντων ὁμόσε στόματ᾽ ἔτραπε Φοῖβος
          Ἀπόλλων,
ἐννῆμαρ δ᾽ ἐς τεῖχος ἵει ῥόον· ὗε δ᾽ ἄρα Ζεὺς
συνεχές, ὄφρα κε θᾶσσον ἁλίπλοα τείχεα θείη.
                                        (12.10–26)

As long as Hektor was still alive and Achilles still
      wrathful
and the city of lord Priam remained unsacked,
for so long did the great wall of the Achaeans also
      remain steadfast.
But when all the best of the Trojans had died,
and many of the Argives were crushed, and some
      were left,
and the city of Priam was sacked in the tenth year,
and the Argives returned in their ships to their dear
      homeland,
then finally Poseidon and Apollo contrived to
      destroy
the wall, sending the strength of rivers against it:
as many as flow from the mountains of Ida to the sea,
Rhesos and Heptaporos and Karesos and Rhodios
and Grenikos and Aisepos and brilliant Skamandros
and Simoeis, where many ox-hide shields and
      helmets
fell in the dust, and the race of the demigods.
Of all these rivers Phoibos Apollo turned the mouths
      together,

and for nine days he hurled their stream against
the wall,
and Zeus rained unceasingly, to dissolve the wall
more quickly into the sea.

The *Iliad* echoes here a myth of destruction that is reflected in both the *Cypria* and the Hesiodic *Ehoeae*—in
which Zeus is said to have planned the Trojan War in
order to destroy the demigods, so as to widen the breach
between gods and men; it is prominent as well in Near
Eastern traditions that make the Flood the means of de-
stroying mankind.[19]

Yet the Homeric poems, as this study began by observing, are interpreters of their mythological resources
at every step; and "destruction" as understood by the
traditions represented by Hesiod, the Cycle, and Mesopotamian literature has been reinterpreted by the *Iliad*
and translated into its own terms. The *Iliad* evokes these
traditions, through passages that retrieve the theme of
destruction, to place them ultimately in a perspective

19. R. Scodel, "Achaean Wall and Myth of Destruction," provides a convincing demonstration of the *Iliad*'s evocation of the
myth. See frag. 204 Merkelbach-West for the Hesiodic reflection
of the myth.

For the Babylonian epic of Atra-ḫasīs, see W. G. Lambert and
A. R. Millard, *Atra-hasis: The Babylonian Story of the Flood* (Ox-
ford, 1969); also J. B. Pritchard, ed., *Ancient Near Eastern Texts,*
2d ed. (Princeton 1955). Among the increasingly rich and valu-
able studies of the interconnections between Near Eastern and
Greek mythology and literature, see now especially W. Burkert,
Die orientalisierende Epoche in der griechischen Religion und Literatur
(Heidelberg, 1984), in particular 85ff.

that, much as it rejects immortality, rejects utter anni-
hilation as well.

Components of the mythological complex of the end
of the race survive in Iliadic allusions, and reverberate,
but are transformed. Thetis's marriage to a mortal is
central to the *Iliad,* not as it is to the *Cypria,* as an instrument in the wholesale eradication of heroes—not to
efface human beings from a crowded landscape—but as a
paradigmatic explanation of why human beings, in order
not to threaten to be greater than their divine parents,
must die. The themes of separation of men and gods,
of human calamity, are not—in G. S. Kirk's phrase—
"watered down" by the *Iliad,* but are distilled.[20] The
plan of Zeus is there, but it is the plan agreed upon by
Zeus and Thetis to honor her short-lived son, the demi-
god, before he dies. Earth's complaint requesting that
her load be lightened is rendered by the *Iliad* in Achilles'
anguished self-reproach that he is an ἄχθος ἀρούρης
(*achthos aroures,* 18.104)—a burden to the earth. Destruction means not the decimation of humanity, but the
shattering loss and sorrow that inescapably define the
life of every individual.

20. G. S. Kirk, "Greek Mythology: Some New Perspec-
tives," *JHS* 92 (1972): 79. Kirk writes: "The 'plan of Zeus' at the
beginning of the *Iliad* was probably in origin a reflexion of the
Mesopotamian or Egyptian gods' recurrent itch to destroy man-
kind; the *Cypria* preserved the idea, but in the *Iliad* this un-
Hellenic conception is in process of being watered down into
Zeus's more limited intention of gratifying Thetis by avenging
Achilles."

Bibliography

(An index to the abbreviations of journal names may be found in *L'Année Philologique*.)

Alexiou, M. *The Ritual Lament in Greek Tradition*. Cambridge, 1974.

Allen, T. W., ed. *Hymns, Epic Cycle*. Vol. 5 of *Homeri Opera*. Oxford, 1912.

————, ed. *Odyssey*. Vols. 3 and 4 of *Homeri opera*. 2d ed. Oxford, 1917, 1919.

Andreae, B., and H. Flashar. "Strukturaequivalenzen zwischen den homerischen Epen und der frühgriechischen Vasenkunst." *Poetica* 9 (1977): 217–65.

Arend, W. *Die typischen Szenen bei Homer*. Berlin, 1933.

Armstrong, J. I. "The Arming Motif in the *Iliad*." *AJP* 79 (1958): 337–54.

Arthur, M. "Politics and Pomegranates: An Interpretation of the Homeric Hymn to Demeter." *Arethusa* 10.1 (Spring 1977): 7–47.

Auerbach, E. *Mimesis*. Princeton, 1953.

Austin, N. "The Function of Digressions in the *Iliad*." *GRBS* 7, no. 4 (1966): 295–312.

Bacon, H. "Aeschylus." In *Ancient Writers: Greece and Rome*, edited by T. J. Luce, vol. 1, 99–155. New York, 1982.

Benveniste, E. "La doctrine médicale des Indo-Européens." *RHR* 130 (1945): 5–12.

————. *Le vocabulaire des institutions indo-européennes I, II*. Paris, 1969.

Bergren, A. L. *The Etymology and Usage of ΠΕΙΡΑΡ in Early Greek Poetry*. American Classical Studies 2, American Philological Association. New York, 1975.

Boedeker, D. D. *Aphrodite's Entry into Greek Epic*. Leiden, 1974.

Bouvier, D. "Mourir près des fontaines de Troie." *Euphrosyne* n.s. 15 (1987): 9–29.

Bowra, C. M. *Homer.* New York, 1972.

———, trans. *The Odes of Pindar.* Harmondsworth, England, 1969.

———. *Pindar.* Oxford, 1964.

———. *Pindari Carmina cum fragmentis.* 2d ed. Oxford, 1947; reprint 1961.

———. *Tradition and Design in the* Iliad. Oxford, 1930; reprint, 1963.

Braswell, B. K. "Mythological Innovation in the *Iliad.*" *CQ* 21 (1971): 16–26.

Brown, N. O., ed. and trans. *Hesiod: Theogony.* Indianapolis, 1953; reprint, 1981.

Buffière, F. *Les mythes d'Homère et la pensée grecque.* Paris, 1956.

Burkert, W. *Die orientalisierende Epoche in der griechischen Religion und Literatur.* Heidelberg, 1984.

———. "Elysion." *Glotta* 39 (1961): 208–13.

———. *Greek Religion.* Cambridge, Mass., 1985.

Calame, C., ed. *Alcman.* Rome, 1983.

Cantilena, M. *Ricerche sulla dizione epica.* Rome, 1982.

Chantraine, P. *Histoire des mots.* Vols. 1–4 of *Dictionnaire étymologique de la langue grecque.* Paris, 1968–80.

Clark, M. E., and W. D. E. Coulson. "Memnon and Sarpedon." *MH* 35 (1978): 65–73.

Clay, J. S. *The Politics of Olympus.* Princeton, 1989.

Coldstream, N. "Hero-Cults in the Age of Homer." *JHS* 96 (1976): 8–17.

Collins, L. *Studies in Characterization in the* Iliad. Beiträge zur klassischen Philologie 189. Frankfurt, 1988.

Conacher, D. J. *Aeschylus'* Prometheus Bound: *A Literary Commentary.* Toronto, 1980.

Coomaraswamy, A. K. "The Darker Side of Dawn." *Smithsonian Miscellaneous Collection* 94.1 (1935): 1–18.

Davies, M. "The Judgement of Paris and *Iliad* XXIV." *JHS* 101 (1981): 56–62.

Detienne, M. *Dionysos mis à mort.* Paris, 1977.

Detienne, M., and J.-P. Vernant. *Les ruses de l'intelligence: La Métis des grecs.* Paris, 1974.

Dietrich, B. C. "The Judgment of Zeus." *RhM* 107 (1964): 97–125.

Dihle, A. *Homer-Probleme*. Opladen, 1970.

Drachmann, A. B., ed. *Scholia vetera in Pindari carmina*. 3 vols. Leipzig, 1903.

Duchemin, J. "Contribution à l'histoire des mythes grecs: les Luttes primordiales dans l'*Iliade* à la lumière des sources proche-orientales." In *Φιλίας Χάριν: Miscellanea di studi classici in onore di Eugenio Manni,* edited by M. Fontana, M. Piraino and F. Rizzo, vol. 3. 837–79. Rome, 1980.

Dumézil, G. *Mitra-Varuna*. 2d ed. Paris, 1948. Published in English, trans. D. Coltman, New York, 1988.

———. *Ouranos-Varuna: Étude de mythologie comparée indo-européenne*. Paris, 1934.

Edmunds, S. *Homeric* Nēpios. New York, 1990.

Edwards, G. P. *The Language of Hesiod in Its Traditional Context*. Oxford, 1971.

Edwards, M. "Homer and the Oral Tradition: The Formula, Part I." *Oral Tradition* 1/2 (1986): 171–230.

———. "Homer and the Oral Tradition: The Formula, Part II." *Oral Tradition* 3/1–2 (1988): 11–60.

———. "Some Stylistic Notes on *Iliad* XVIII." *AJP* 89 (1968): 257–83.

———. "Type-scenes and Homeric Hospitality." *TAPA* 105 (1975): 51–72.

Eliade, M. *Images and Symbols*. Translated by P. Mairet. New York, 1969.

Erbse, H., ed. *Scholia Graeca in Homeri Iliadem*. 7 vols. Berlin, 1969–77.

Felson-Rubin, N. "Penelope's Perspectives: Character from Plot." In *Beyond Oral Poetry,* edited by J. M. Bremer, I. J. F. de Jong, and J. Kalff, 61–83. Amsterdam, 1987.

Fenik, B. Iliad *X and the* Rhesus: *The Myth*. Brussels, 1964.

———. *Typical Battle Scenes in the* Iliad: *Studies in the Narrative Technique of Homeric Battle Description*. Hermes Einzelschriften 21. Wiesbaden, 1968.

Finley, J. H., Jr. *Pindar and Aeschylus*. 1955; reprint, Cambridge, Mass., 1966.

Fittschen, K. *Untersuchungen zum Beginn der Sagendarstellungen bei den Griechen*. Berlin, 1969.

Frame, D. *The Myth of Return in Early Greek Epic*. New Haven, 1978.

Friedrich, P. *The Meaning of Aphrodite*. Chicago, 1978.

Friedrich, R. *Stilwandel im homerischen Epos: Studien zur Poetik und Theorie der epischen Gattung*. Heidelberg, 1975.

Fritz, K. von. "Greek Prayers." *The Review of Religion* 10 (1945): 5–39.

Gaisser, J. H. "Adaptation of Traditional Material in the Glaucos-Diomedes Episode." *TAPA* 100 (1969): 165–76.

———. "A Structural Analysis of the Digressions in the *Iliad* and the *Odyssey*." *HSCP* 73 (1968): 1–43.

Greengard, C. *The Structure of Pindar's Epinician Odes*. Amsterdam, 1980.

Griffin, J. "The Epic Cycle and the Uniqueness of Homer." *JHS* 97 (1977): 39–53.

Griffith, J. G. "The Myth of Lycurgus, King of the Edonian Thracians, in Literature and Art." In *Ancient Bulgaria*. International Symposium on the Ancient History and Archaeology of Bulgaria. Nottingham, 1983.

Griffith, M. *Aeschylus: Prometheus Bound*. Cambridge, 1983.

Hainsworth, J. B. *The Flexibility of the Homeric Formula*. Oxford, 1968.

———. *Homer*. Oxford, 1969.

Heubeck, A. *Die homerische Frage*. Darmstadt, 1974; reprint, 1988.

———. "Mythologische Vorstellungen des Alten Orients im archaischen Griechentum." *Gymnasium* 62 (1955): 508–25.

Hoekstra, A. *Homeric Modifications of Formulaic Prototypes: Studies in the Development of Greek Epic Diction*. Amsterdam, 1964.

Hooker, J. T. "ΑΙΓΑΙΩΝ in Achilles' Plea to Thetis." *JHS* 100 (1980): 188–89.

Howald, E. *Der Dichter der* Ilias. Erlenbach-Zurich, 1946.

———. *Der Mythos als Dichtung*. Zurich, 1937.

Huxley, G. L. *Greek Epic Poetry: From Eumelos to Panyassis*. London, 1969.

Ingalls, W. B. "Linguistic and Formular Innovation in the Mythological Digressions in the *Iliad*." *Phoenix* 36 (1982): 201–8.

Janko, R. *Homer, Hesiod and the Hymns: Diachronic Development in Epic Diction*. Cambridge, 1982.

———. *The* Iliad: *A Commentary*. Vol. IV: *Books 13–16*. Cambridge, 1992.

Johansen, K. F. *The Iliad in Early Greek Art*. Copenhagen, 1967.

Kaiser, J. *Peleus und Thetis: Eine sagengeschichtliche Untersuchung.* Munich, 1912.

Kakridis, J. Th. *Homeric Researches.* Lund, 1949.

———. *Homer Revisited.* Lund, 1971.

Kakridis, Ph. J. "Achilleus Rüstung." *Hermes* 89 (1961): 288–97.

King, K. C. *Achilles: Paradigms of the War Hero from Homer to the Middle Ages.* Berkeley, 1987.

Kirk, G. S. "Greek Mythology: Some New Perspectives." *JHS* 92 (1972): 74–85.

———, ed. *The Iliad: A Commentary.* Cambridge, 1985.

Köhnken, A. "Gods and Descendants of Aiakos in Pindar's Eighth Isthmian Ode." *BICS* 22 (1975): 25–36.

———. "Die Narbe des Odysseus: Ein Beitrag zur homerisch-epischen Erzähltechnik." *AuA* 22.2 (1976): 101–14.

Koller, H. "Das kitharodische Prooimion: Eine formgeschichtliche Untersuchung." *Philologus* 100 (1956): 159–206.

Krischer, T. *Formale Konventionen der homerischen Epik.* Munich, 1971.

Kullmann, W. *Die Quellen der* Ilias *(Troischer Sagenkreis).* Hermes Einzelschriften 14. Wiesbaden, 1960.

———. "Ein vorhomerisches Motiv im Iliasproömium." *Philologus* 99 (1955): 167–92.

———. "Zur ΔΙΟΣ ΒΟΥΛΗ des Iliasproömiums." *Philologus* 100 (1956): 132–33.

———. "Zur Methode der Neoanalyse in der Homerforschung." *Wiener Studien* n.s. 15 (1981): 5–42.

Lambert, W. G., and A. R. Millard. *Atra-ḫasīs: The Babylonian Story of the Flood.* Oxford, 1969.

Lang, M. L. "Reason and Purpose in Homeric Prayers." *CW* 68 (1975): 309–14.

———. "Reverberations and Mythology in the *Iliad.*" In *Approaches to Homer,* edited by C. A. Rubino and C. W. Shelmerdine, 140–64. Austin, 1983.

Leaf, W., ed. *The Iliad.* 2 vols. 2d ed. London, 1900, 1902.

Lesky, A. "Peleus und Thetis im frühen Epos." In *Gesammelte Schriften,* 401–9. Bern, 1966.

———. *RE* 19.1 (1937), 271–308, s.v. "Peleus."

Lévi-Strauss, C. *The Raw and the Cooked.* New York, 1969; reprint, 1975.

Littleton, S. "The 'Kingship in Heaven' Theme." In *Myth and Law among the Indo-Europeans,* edited by J. Puhvel, 83–121. Berkeley, 1970.

Lobel, E., ed. *POxy.* 24. London, 1957. No. 2390. Frag. 2.

Lohmann, D. *Die Komposition der Reden der* Ilias. Berlin, 1970.

Loraux, N. "*Hèbè* et *andreia.* Deux versions de la mort du combattant athénien." *Ancient Society* 6 (1975): 1–31.

————. *Façons tragiques de tuer une femme.* Paris, 1985.

————. *Les expériences de Tirésias: Le féminin et l'homme grec.* Paris, 1989.

————. *Les Mères en Deuil.* Paris, 1990.

Lord, A. "Composition by Theme in Homer and Southslavic Epos." *TAPA* 82 (1951): 71–80.

————. *The Singer of Tales.* Cambridge, Mass., 1960. Reprint, New York, 1965.

Lowenstam, S. *The Death of Patroklos: A Study in Typology.* Beiträge zur klassischen Philologie 133. Königstein, 1981.

Ludwich, A. *Textkritische Untersuchungen über die mythologischen Scholien zu Homers* Ilias. Vol. 1. Königsberg, 1900.

Lung, G. E. "Memnon: Archäologische Studien zur *Aethiopis.*" Diss., Bonn, 1912.

MacCary, W. T. *Childlike Achilles: Ontogeny and Phylogeny in the* Iliad. New York, 1982.

Mawet, F. *Le vocabulaire homérique de la douleur.* Brussels, 1979.

Merkelbach, R. "ΚΟΡΟΣ." *ZPE* 8 (1971): 80.

Meyer, H. "Hymnische Stilelemente in der frühgriechischen Dichtung." Diss., Cologne, 1933.

Monro, D. B., ed. *Odyssey.* 2 vols. Oxford, 1901.

Monro, D. B., and T. W. Allen, eds. *Iliad.* Vols. 1 and 2 of *Homeri opera.* 3d ed. Oxford, 1920.

Most, G. "Alcman's 'Cosmogonic' Fragment (Fr. 5 Page, 81 Calame)." *CQ* 37, no. 1 (1987): 1–19.

Muellner, L. C. *The Meaning of Homeric EYXOMAI through its Formulas.* Innsbruck, 1976.

Murray, G. *The Rise of the Greek Epic.* 4th ed. Oxford, 1934; reprint, 1961.

Nagler, M. "Dread Goddess Endowed with Speech." *Archaeological News* 6 (1977): 77–85.

————. *Spontaneity and Tradition: A Study in the Oral Art of Homer.* Berkeley, 1974.

————. "Towards a Generative View of the Oral Formula." *TAPA* 98 (1967): 269–311.

Nagy, G. *The Best of the Achaeans.* Baltimore, 1979.

————. *Comparative Studies of Greek and Indic Meter.* Cambridge, Mass., 1974.

————. *Greek Mythology and Poetics.* Ithaca, N.Y., 1990.

Neschke-Hentschke, A. "Geschichten und Geschichte: Zum Beispiel Prometheus bei Hesiod und Aischylos." *Hermes* 111 (1983): 385–402.

Norden, E. *Agnostos Theos.* Leipzig, 1913.

Notopoulos, J. A. "Studies in Early Greek Poetry." *HSCP* 68 (1964): 1–77.

Page, D. L. *The Homeric Odyssey.* Oxford, 1955.

————, ed. *Poetae Melici Graeci.* Oxford, 1962.

Parry, A., ed. *The Making of Homeric Verse.* Oxford, 1971.

Parry, M. *L'épithète traditionelle dans Homère.* Paris, 1928.

————. "Studies in the Epic Technique of Oral Versemaking." *HSCP* 41 (1930): 73–147.

Pestalozzi, H. *Die Achilleis als Quelle der Ilias.* Erlenbach-Zurich, 1945.

Petegorsky, D. *Context and Evocation: Studies in Early Greek and Sanskrit Poetry.* Ann Arbor, Mich., 1982.

————. "Demeter and the Black Robe of Grief." Unpublished paper.

Postlethwaite, N. "Formula and Formulaic: Some Evidence from the Homeric Hymns." *Phoenix* 33 (1979): 1–18.

Pötscher, W. "Hera und Heros." *RhM* 104 (1961): 302–55.

Price, Th. Hadzisteliou. "Hero-Cult and Homer." *Historia* 22 (1973): 129–44.

Pritchard, J. B., ed. *Ancient Near Eastern Texts.* 2d ed. Princeton, 1955.

Privitera, G. A. *Dionisio in Omero e nella poesia greca arcaica.* Rome, 1970.

Ramnoux, C. *Mythologie ou la famille olympienne.* Paris, 1959.

Redfield, J. "The Proem of the *Iliad:* Homer's Art." *Classical Philology* 74 (1979): 95–110.

Reinhardt, K. "Das Parisurteil." In *Tradition und Geist,* 16–36. Göttingen, 1960.

————. *Der* Ilias *und ihr Dichter.* Göttingen, 1961.

Reitzenstein, R. "Die Hochzeit des Peleus und der Thetis." *Hermes* 35 (1900): 73–105.

Richardson, N. J., ed. *The Homeric Hymn to Demeter.* Oxford, 1974; reprint, 1979.

Rohde, E. *Psyche: Seelencult und Unsterblichkeitsglaube der Griechen.* 2 vols. Freiburg, 1898; 4th ed., Tübingen, 1907. Translated by W. B. Hillis. New York, 1925; reprint, 1966.

Russo, J. "The Structural Formula in Homeric Verse." *YCS* 20 (1966): 217–40.

Sachs, E. "Die Meleagererzählung in der *Ilias* und das mythische Paradeigma." *Philologus* 88 (1933): 16–29.

Sacks, R. *The Traditional Phrase in Homer: Two Studies in Form, Meaning, and Interpretation.* Leiden, 1987.

Schadewaldt, W. *Von Homers Welt und Werk.* 2d ed. Stuttgart, 1952.

Schefold, K. *Myth and Legend in Early Greek Art.* London, 1966.

Schein, S. L. *The Mortal Hero: An Introduction to Homer's* Iliad. Berkeley, 1984.

Schmidt, E. G. "Himmel—Meer—Erde im frühgriechischen Epos und im Alten Orient." *Philologus* 125 (1981): 1–24.

Schmitt, R. *Dichtung und Dichtersprache in indogermanischer Zeit.* Wiesbaden, 1967.

Schneider, A. *Der troische Sagenkreis in der ältesten griechischen Kunst.* Leipzig, 1886.

Schoeck, G. Ilias *und* Aethiopis: *Kyklische Motive in homerischer Brechung.* Zurich, 1961.

Scodel, R. "The Achaean Wall and the Myth of Destruction." *HSCP* 86 (1982): 33–50.

Segal, C. P. "Greek Myth as a Semiotic and Structural System and the Problem of Tragedy." *Arethusa* 16 (1983): 173–98.

————. "The Homeric Hymn to Aphrodite: A Structuralist Approach." *CW* 67 (1974): 205–12.

————. *The Theme of the Mutilation of the Corpse in the* Iliad. Leiden, 1971.

Severyns, A. *Le cycle épique dans l'école d'Aristarque.* Liège, 1928.

————. "Recherches sur la *Chrestomathie* de Proclus." *Bibliothè-*

que de la Faculté de Philosophie et Lettres de l'Université de Liège, fasc. 170 (1963): 76–85.

———. "Sur le début des chants cypriens." *Mededelingen der Koninklijke Nederlandse Akademie van Wetenschappen, afd. Letterkunde* n.s. 28, no. 5 (1965): 285–97.

Shannon, R. *The Arms of Achilles and Homeric Compositional Technique.* Leiden, 1975.

Sheppard, J. T. *The Pattern of the* Iliad. London, 1922.

Sinos, D. *Achilles, Patroklos, and the Meaning of* Philos. Innsbruck, 1980.

Slatkin, L. M. "Genre and Generation in the *Odyssey.*" *MHTIΣ* 1, no. 2 (1986): 259–68.

———. "Les amis mortels." *L'écrit du temps* 19 (1988): 119–32.

———. "The Wrath of Thetis." *TAPA* 116 (1986): 1–24.

Smith, P. M. "Aeneidai as Patrons of *Iliad* XX and the Homeric *Hymn to Aphrodite.*" *HSCP* 85 (1981): 17–58.

Solmsen, F. *Hesiod and Aeschylus.* Ithaca, N.Y., 1949.

Stoessl, F. *Die Trilogie des Aischylos: Formgesetze und Wege der Rekonstruktion.* Baden bei Wien, 1937.

Stolz, B., and R. Shannon, eds. *Oral Theory and the Formula.* Ann Arbor, Mich., 1976.

Thomson, G. *Aeschylus: The Prometheus Bound.* Cambridge, 1932.

Vernant, J.-P. "Thétis et le poème cosmogonique d'Alcman." In *Hommages à Marie Delcourt,* 38–69. Collection Latomus 114. Brussels, 1970.

Vidal-Naquet, P. "Le chasseur noir et l'origine de l'éphébie athénienne." *Économies-sociétés-civilisations* 23 (1968): 947–64.

Watkins, C. "À propos de MHNIΣ." *BSL* 72 (1977): 187–209. Translated as "On MHNIΣ." *Indo-European Studies* 3 (1977): 686–722.

West, M. L. "Alcman and Pythagoras." *CQ* 61 (1967): 1–7.

———. *Early Greek Philosophy and the Orient.* Oxford, 1971.

———. "Three Presocratic Cosmologies." *CQ* 57, n.s. 13 (1963): 154–76.

———, ed. *Hesiod: Theogony.* Oxford, 1966.

Whitman, C. H. *Homer and the Heroic Tradition.* Cambridge, Mass., 1958.

Wilamowitz-Moellendorf, U. von. *Aischylos Interpretationen.* Berlin, 1914.

————, ed. *Euripides: Herakles.* 1895; reprint, Bad Homburg, 1959.

Willcock, M. "Ad Hoc Invention in the *Iliad.*" *HSCP* 81 (1977): 41–53.

————. "Mythological Paradeigma in the *Iliad.*" *CQ* 58, n.s. 14 (1964): 141–54.

Wust, E. *RE* 23.2 (1959), 1439–58, s.v. "Psychostasie."

Index

133

Compositor: G&S Typesetters, Inc.
Text: 10½ × 14½ Bembo
Display: Bembo
Printer: Braun-Brumfield, Inc.
Binder: Braun-Brumfield, Inc.